To Roger
With deep regard
and thanksgiving
for your ministry,
Steve

JESUS STORIES

TRAVELING TOWARD TESTIMONY

H. STEPHEN SHOEMAKER
FOREWORD BY BILL J. LEONARD

D1596365

JUDSON PRESS
PUBLISHERS SINCE 1824
VALLEY FORGE, PA

JESUS STORIES: TRAVELING TOWARD TESTIMONY

Interior design by Crystal Devine.
Cover photo © iStockphoto, cover design by David Shoemaker

Library of Congress Cataloging-in-Publication Data

Cataloging-in-Publication Data available upon request.
Contact cip@judsonpress.com.

Printed in the U.S.A.

First printing, 2016.

TO ALL THOSE

WHO HAVE PASSED

THE STORY OF JESUS

ON TO ME

CONTENTS

PART IV: THE LAST AND FIRST DAYS

PART V: CONCLUSIONS

FOREWORD

"How God anointed Jesus of Nazareth with the Holy Ghost and with power; who went about doing good and healing all those that were oppressed by the devil; for God was with him." —Simon Peter (Acts 10:38)

"And in one Lord Jesus Christ, the only-begotten of the Father before all worlds; God of God, Light of Light, very God of very God; begotten, not made, being of one substance with the Father, by whom all things were made." —Nicene Creed

"Nobody knows the trouble I've seen. Nobody knows but Jesus." —Spiritual

"Jesus had a way of talking soft and outside of a few bankers and higher-ups among the con men of Jerusalem everybody liked to have this Jesus around . . . and he helped the sick and gave the people hope." —Carl Sandburg, "To a Contemporary Bunk Shooter"
"Jesus is a good guy." —Bill Maher

On reading this fine book *Jesus Stories: Traveling toward Testimony*, by my longtime friend and former pastor Steve Shoemaker, I recalled a conversation about Jesus between former president Jimmy Carter and comedian/commentator Bill Maher. The setting was Maher's "Real Time" broadcast on HBO, March 28, 2014. Carter was there to highlight the publication of his twenty-eighth book, *A Call to Action: Women, Religion, Violence and Power*.

Acknowledging the continued global violence against women, Maher noted the use of sacred texts in defending, even encouraging, such abusive actions. He then asked Carter why certain religionists cite their respective scriptures as giving them permission to treat females in violent, dehumanizing ways. While admitting that scripture can be used variously,

Carter confessed that after decades of teaching Sunday school, when he "gets into trouble" with texts, "I go back to what Jesus said, and I don't find anything that violates my principles." Maher, no friend to organized religion, conceded that "Jesus is a good guy." President Carter read sacred texts *through* Jesus, and even Bill Maher had to agree that adding Jesus to the discussion raised it to a whole new level.

In *Jesus Stories*, Steve Shoemaker goes "back to what Jesus said," offering insights into the importance of the man from Nazareth who became for the church the Christ of God. As Shoemaker sees it, retelling the Jesus story, necessary in every era, is particularly essential for articulating and shaping twenty-first century Christian faith.

First and foremost, the *stories* remind us who Jesus is, what he said, and how he lived as a timeless witness to and vehicle of God's grace. Jesus was and remains an arresting figure whose ideas and actions are specific and expansive, global and personal all at once. In fact, the stories are so dynamic that we may hear them differently at various stages of our lives. Stories we have heard repeatedly suddenly find us as if we had never heard them before.

Second, given momentous changes in the contemporary religious landscape, a growing segment of the population may actually know very little about Jesus, his life, and his teaching. Declines in church attendance mirror national surveys suggesting that one of five people in the United States claim no religious affiliation ("Nones"). Because their actual knowledge of Jesus may be limited, some readers may confront specifics of the Jesus story for the first time ever.

Third, even those of us who think we know the stories may often take them for granted, or become so comfortable with them that we overlook their real power to transform us, challenge us, or carry us where we do not want to go. In this book Shoemaker compels us to revisit Jesus who calls human beings to live before God and with one another. It is a journey worth taking or retaking, then and there, here and now.

Fourth, in creative and provocative ways, Shoemaker carries us through the Gospel texts, linking them with theology, literature, history, and the life of the Spirit. Thus *Jesus Stories* becomes an excellent resource for instructing Christians old and new in the details and varied meanings of the Gospel stories. This is a fine work of biblical scholarship punctuated by pastoral and personal implications within the texts. As such, it is a valuable resource for spiritual formation.

Finally, *Jesus Stories* calls readers to engage in a personal quest for Jesus himself, who he was and who he remains, from the manger-child to the controversial prophet-teacher; from the crucified martyr to the risen Savior. The stories, like Jesus himself, occupy a first-century context that at times seems exceedingly distant and distinct from our twenty-first century lives. But they are also timeless guides to God's continuing grace, known profoundly when "the Word became flesh and dwelt among us." *Jesus Stories* reminds us yet again that, whether we are looking for God or not, God is looking for us. Good news, right?

Bill J. Leonard, MDiv, PhD
James and Marilyn Dunn Professor of Baptist Studies
Professor of Church History
Wake Forest University

PREFACE

The Jesus Story is one of the foundational stories of the world. And yet, it is so easily hijacked by those who wish to use it for their own purposes. It is a perennial temptation for us all: to take the story whose power is the saving, healing, liberating power of God and use it to serve our small, self-justifying, ego-driven stories.

Noted Roman Catholic scholar Romano Guardini asked, "Who can protect Jesus from us? Who will keep him free from the cunning and violence of our own ego?"[1] The story of Jesus belongs to the world and to God. The church is the steward of the story, but neither the church nor any other institution or individual controls the story.

The Jesus Story encompasses what we call "the historical Jesus,"[2] but there's more to Jesus than the historical Jesus. Hence the Jesus Story includes what I will call the "more-than-historical Jesus," the Jesus remembered and experienced as the Living One. History is here but more than history, there is story, song, and poetry: the native tongue of religion.

I set out to tell the story of Jesus, making use of current historical research on the man, Jesus of Nazareth. I also draw on the Jesus remembered in the four canonical Gospels and the Jesus experienced in the Spirit of God from the resurrection on. It is inevitably "*my* gospel" that I tell, to use Paul's phrase (Romans 16:25), but I hope it will be faithful to *the* gospel that has transformed lives and transfigured history.

In a 1986 PBS program on the Bible, Bill Moyers said that we need to take the Bible back from the biblical experts and religious extremists. In much the same way, we need to take Jesus back too. As for the experts, Moyers was not being dismissive of good scholarship, but referring to those scholars who would hold our Bible for us and tell us exactly what it means. Moyers is interested, as I am, in getting scholars and the general public together for a direct conversation about Jesus.

Albert Schweitzer, who took on the project of reviewing Jesus scholarship to his time, wrote this warning and confession:

> We modern theologians are too proud of our historical method, too proud of our historical Jesus, too confident in our belief in the spiritual gains which our historical theology can bring to the world. . . . There was a danger of thrusting ourselves between men and the Gospels, and refusing to leave the individual man alone with the sayings of Jesus. There was a danger that we should offer them a Jesus who was too small because we had forced Him into conformity with our human standards and human psychology.[3]

As for the extremists, they are everywhere. The Bible has been hijacked by extremists who use it to justify hatred and "sacred violence" done in the name of God. Every religion has its extremists. Many people today view Christianity as a religion of bigotry, violence, and exclusion, all in the name of Jesus, who himself welcomed all people into the kingdom of God and taught us to love not only our neighbor, but our enemies as well. As W. H. Auden put it:

You shall love your crooked neighbor
With your crooked heart.[4]

Part of the context of this book is the fourteen years I served as senior minister of Myers Park Baptist Church in Charlotte, North Carolina, a progressive American Baptist congregation. During those years, we invited New Testament scholars, historians, and theologians to help us on our quest for who Jesus was and is. Among those who spent weekends with us were such luminary thinkers as Marcus Borg, John

Dominic Crossan, Amy-Jill Levine, N. T. Wright, Elaine Pagels, Bart Ehrman, Stanley Hauerwas, John Shelby Spong, Sandra Schneiders, Roger Haight, Harvey Cox, Serene Jones, and Cynthia Bourgeault.[5] It has not been dull.

John Meier, a Roman Catholic New Testament scholar, has proposed a fanciful thought experiment on how to get to the core of who the historical Jesus was: gather a Protestant scholar, a Roman Catholic scholar, an agnostic scholar, and a Jewish scholar. Place them in a room in the basement of the Harvard Divinity School library. Tell them they cannot come out until they have arrived at a consensus document.[6] (I hope someone is bringing in food and water.)

We have had at Myers Park Baptist that full array of scholars spanning a wide theological spectrum. No consensus has been reached, but those weekends have energized and instructed us in our quest for who Jesus was and is.

Those weekends have also taught me the limits of historical research. Knowledge of the historical Jesus is essential to Christian faith, but it is not enough. Its tools are finite; its reach is not long enough.

The story of Jesus is far more than the documented history of Jesus we can recover. So our quest for the historical Jesus is joined with a quest for the more-than-historical Jesus, a Jesus alive to us in the Spirit of God—a Jesus in search of us.

Is there a Jesus spiritually accessible to us? And if so, how is this Jesus connected to the first-century man of Galilee? Such are the questions that occupy me as I offer you the Jesus stories in this book. What we are about goes beyond historical reconstruction; we are about spiritual transformation.

NOTES

1. As cited in Gerhard Lohfink, *Jesus of Nazareth: What He Wanted, Who He Was*, trans. Linda M. Maloney (Collegeville, MN: Liturgical Press, 2012), 18.

2. By "historical Jesus," I mean those scholarly reconstructions of who the man Jesus of Nazareth was, based on the records that historians have access to.

3. Albert Schweitzer, *The Quest of the Historical Jesus: A Critical Study of Its Progress from Reimarus to Wrede* (Baltimore: Johns Hopkins University Press, with the Albert Schweitzer Institute, 1998), 400. This book was originally published as

Von Reimarus zu Wrede: Eine Geschichte der Leben-Jesu-Forschung (Tübingen: Mohr, 1906).

4. W. H. Auden, "As I Walked Out One Evening," in W. H. Auden, *Collected Poems*, ed. Edward Mendelson (New York: Random House, 1976), 115.

5. These are among the most noted current Jesus scholars, theologians, and historians, including some prominent members of the acclaimed and vilified Jesus Seminar.

6. John P. Meier, *A Marginal Jew: Rethinking the Historical Jesus*, vol. 1, *The Roots of the Problem and the Person* (New York: Doubleday, 1990), 1–2.

ACKNOWLEDGMENTS

A proper list of acknowledgments could go on and on, so grateful am I. I begin with thanks to all who have passed the story of Jesus on to me: persons such as my mother and father; churches that raised me and with which I've ministered; schools such as Stetson University, Union Theological Seminary (New York), and the Southern Baptist Theological Seminary and my teachers there. I mention two in particular: George A. Buttrick and J. Louis Martyn.

I thank the Collegeville Institute for Ecumenical and Cultural Research and its director, Dr. Donald Ottenhoff, for inviting me to be a resident scholar, where I did major research and writing for this book. I thank Myers Park Baptist Church in Charlotte, North Carolina, which I served as senior minister, and whose annual series of workshops, "Jesus in the Twenty-first Century," brought many of the leading Jesus scholars for weekends of lectures. And I thank Amy R. Jones, whose thoughtful and skillful production of the manuscript made this a better book.

Lastly, or firstly, I thank you, Lord, whose earthly life and present spirit have shaped and are shaping my life.

INTRODUCTION

"I Stop Here Waiting for You"

I invite you to join me on a quest as we search for the Jesus in search of us. There is the "historical Jesus," the figure who lived in first-century CE Galilee, as best we can reconstruct. And there is the "more-than-historical Jesus," who is alive to us in the Spirit of God.

The modern quest for the historical Jesus is important to correct false and fanciful pictures of Jesus that distort the true meaning of Christian faith. The quest for the more-than-historical Jesus is important because it has to do with the Risen Christ as the ongoing presence of God in our lives. To use Harry Emerson Fosdick's categories, there is the "Christ of History" and the "Christ of Experience."[1]

We are on a journey with Jesus toward God, with God, into God. Theologian Roger Haight writes, "Jesus was a person in whom people encountered God. The basis for Jesus' central place in the Christian faith rests in the fact that he continues to be one in whom people encounter God."[2] The early Christians' creeds sought to put into words Jesus' humanity and divinity. Behind the words was the experience of Jesus, genuine humanity and genuine divine presence. That experience continues.

So I offer this two-pronged quest. We are after as clear a picture of the historical Jesus as possible. Yet we are also in pursuit of the more-than-historical Jesus in search of us.

Rabbi Abraham Heschel asserts in his seminal book *God in Search of Man* that the God we pursue is also in pursuit of us.[3] Might Jesus be an embodiment of the holy initiative of God? As the poet Rainer Maria Rilke phrased it, "the One you are looking for is also looking for you."[4] Or, to quote an anonymous hymn from the late nineteenth century:

> *I sought the Lord, and afterward I knew*
> *He moved my soul to seek Him, seeking me.*
> *It was not I that found, O Savior true;*
> *No, I was found of Thee.*

This book is like a mystery novel where the detective in search of a missing person begins to suspect that the person she is looking for not only is alive but also is searching for *her*, and doing so not to bring calamity but rather the best, almost unimaginable, good news.

The modern quest for the historical Jesus began more than two hundred years ago, the child of Enlightenment inquiry. The search for the more-than-historical Jesus is more than two thousand years old, as people have sought to know the Jesus of the Gospels, alive to them in the Spirit of God.

Flannery O'Connor, novelist and astute observer of the religion of the South, wrote, "While the South is hardly Christ-centered, it is more certainly Christ-haunted."[5] I confess to a certain Christ-hauntedness as an unabashed, if stumbling, follower of Jesus—and as one who grew up in a Southern culture that was far from Christ-centered despite its overt Christian religiosity.

I am Christ-haunted because Jesus' way of life seems impossibly demanding. I am Christ-haunted because I am fascinated with him and hungry to know more completely this man who embodied the truth, compassion, and goodness of God, of God's light and life and love. He was and is to me, as to George Buttrick, "surprise of Mercy, outgoing Gladness, Rescue, Healing and Life."[6]

Christ is the intimate one and elusive one, the demanding and forgiving one, the inescapable one. I am tracking Jesus, and he is tracking me.

We have a hunger for "what happened," for the historical. Who was this figure who taught and healed, set free and forgave, who preached God's kingdom drawn graciously and urgently near, the kingdom of justice and joy, mercy and peace? Who was he who befriended sinners and outcasts, brought good news to the poor, and challenged the religious and political status quo to the point that he was *crucifiable*? Who was he who taught the love of enemy and eschewed violence, yet was executed on a Roman cross as an enemy of the state? We want to know more about him, to know him. We want evidence, as the poet Anne Sexton put it, "that the Christ who walked for me / walked on true ground."[7]

There is an urgency and a timeliness to the search. The urgency is that religions of all stripes are making our world a more dangerous place in the early twenty-first century. Geopolitics has become geo-religio-politics. Extremist Islamic terrorists fly suicide missions into the World Trade Towers with praise of Allah on their lips. A U.S. Marine website published a photo of a U.S. tank during the Iraq War, with the words "NEW TESTAMENT" emblazoned on its gun barrel.

There is in the United States today a bewildering and contradictory array of Jesuses being offered: Capitalist Jesus and Social Gospel Jesus; Jesus the Zealot and Jesus the Pacifist; Jesus Savior of Souls and Jesus the Community Organizer; the Jesus of the Prosperity Gospel and the Jesus of the Poor; Justice Jesus and Tea Party Jesus; Jesus of the Right and Jesus of the Left; the Jesus whose sole aim was to get us safely into heaven and the Jesus whose passion was the transformation of earth.

Who *was* he? Who *is* he? Can we enlist him in *any* cause? Are there causes for which he wishes to enlist us? Or, when it comes to the historic Jesus, is there no *there* there, to use the words of Gertrude Stein about Oakland, California?

I believe there is a *there* there, that there are crucial things you can know about Jesus of Nazareth. There are no pictures of Jesus that are not interpretations of Jesus. Jesus was one perceived and remembered, and remembering itself is a form of interpretation.[8] But some interpretations are truer than others, more faithful to the Jesus of history.

And yet there is a *more* there too, a Living Christ, who continues to speak, challenge, heal, empower, and call us to tasks that embody the kingdom of God for our day—the more-than-historical Jesus.

The timeliness of this book is twofold. First is the reopened quest for the historical Jesus, renewed in the 1980s, by scholars' count the third in a succession of quests. It has gathered the attention of the public. There are new discoveries, new scholarly tools, new entry points into our understanding of the Jesus of history.

There has also been an explosion of research and writing on the "noncanonical" (not church approved) and "apocryphal" ("covered over" or "hidden away") Gospels that have been discovered over the last 120 years, of special note being the Nag Hammadi library uncovered in 1945. What was lost, or covered up, is now found. And we are discovering a much greater variety in early Christianities (now seen as plural) than we once thought. We are thinking afresh about the diversity in the unity of Christian faith.

The timeliness also has to do with the spiritual hunger of our age and the drive to find a Jesus less encumbered by centuries of Christian dogma, a Jesus more immediate to our daily lives, a "Jesus spirituality"—Jesus as a spiritual path and practice.

For all the above, we need the historical Jesus and the more-than-historical Jesus. There will be history here, as best as I, with the help of scholars, know it. There will be close attention to Jesus' words as remembered in the New Testament Gospels, and overheard conversations that he had with people, and reflections on his deeds and what was done to him.

There will also be my own ongoing conversation with Jesus, the imagination's work of holy meeting, and glimpses of conversations he has had with those who have followed his path over the last two thousand years.

Finally, there will be me seeking to know Jesus with a form of knowing that is also a form of loving. In Chaim Potok's novel *The Promise*, the main character, Reuven Malter, is a young rabbinical student who loves his tradition but wants to use modern critical tools in his study. When he goes for his final rabbinical exam, his main examiner is his fundamentalist Hasidic teacher, Rev Kalman, who detests modern critical study of texts and tradition. Reuven thinks he is doomed. To his great surprise, Rev Kalman passes him. Afterward, Reuven asks his teacher why. The rabbi responds that he did not want to pass him, that he opposes the use of historical critical tools, but when examining Reuven, he heard the Song of Songs in his voice. (The Song of Songs is the book in the Bible that is an ecstatic love poem that biblical interpreters have long read as analogy for the love between ourselves and God.) The rabbi said:

> "Once I had students who spoke with such love about the Torah that I would hear the Song of Songs in their voices." He spoke softly with his eyes closed. "I have not heard the Song of Songs now for—for—." He blinked. "I did not hear the Song of Songs in America until I heard your voice at the examinations. Not your words, but your voice. I did not like the words. But the voice. . . . Do you understand what I mean, Reuven?"[9]

I employ in this book the scholars' methods, but I seek in the writing of this book a form of knowing that is more than a scholar's knowing, a personal knowing—like the sound of the Song of Songs.

How did I choose what of Jesus' words and deeds to include in this book? Two answers come to mind, the first from

Rilke's poem "Archaic Torso of Apollo." It ends with the words "You must change your life."[10] I write about those places where I have heard the *imperative*: "You must change your life." These encounters with the words, deeds, and spirit of Jesus have not only the force of the imperative, however, but also the power of the indicative: "You can; yes, with God you can."

The second criterion for my selection is *amazement*. Annie Dillard writes, "You were made and set here to give voice to this, your own astonishment."[11] Here in this book are the places in Jesus' life that have brought me astonishment. The Greek word *ekstasis* is close: "beside yourself, out of your everyday mind."

At the end of Walt Whitman's "Song of Myself," he suggests that we the readers may have missed who he is or what he means. He closes:

> *Failing to fetch me at first keep encouraged,*
> *Missing me one place search another.*
> *I stop somewhere waiting for you.*[12]

Jesus says to us, "I stop somewhere waiting for you."

Here is my account of Jesus' life as I am coming to know him in study, worship, halting obedience, and Christian community. It is my testimony, my search, my story, my song. Come join the quest and create your own testimony.

NOTES

1. Harry Emerson Fosdick, *What Is Vital in Religion* (New York: Harper, 1955), 34–45.

2. Roger Haight, *Jesus, Symbol of God* (Maryknoll, NY: Orbis Books, 1999), 87.

3. Abraham Heschel, *God in Search of Man: A Philosophy of Judaism* (New York: Farrar, Straus & Giroux, 1983).

4. As cited in Stephanie Dowrick, *In the Company of Rilke: Why a 20th-Century Poet Speaks So Eloquently to 21st-Century Readers* (New York: Penguin Books, 2011), 9.

5. Flannery O'Connor, *Mystery and Manners*, as cited in Susan Ketchin, *The Christ-Haunted Landscape: Faith and Doubt in Southern Fiction* (Jackson: University Press of Mississippi, 1994), 41.

6. George Arthur Buttrick, *Prayer* (New York: Abingdon-Cokesbury Press, 1942), 83.

7. Anne Sexton, "Frenzy," in Anne Sexton, *The Complete Poems* (Boston: Houghton Mifflin, 1981), 466.

8. See James D. G. Dunn, *Christianity in the* Making, vol. 1, *Jesus Remembered* (Grand Rapids: Eerdmans, 2003); Anthony Le Donne, *Historical Jesus: What Can We Know and How Can We Know It?* (Grand Rapids: Eerdmans, 2011).

9. Chaim Potok, *The Promise* (New York: Anchor Books, 2005), 339–40.

10. Rainer Maria Rilke, "Archaic Torso of Apollo," in Rainer Maria Rilke, *The Selected Poetry of Rainer Maria Rilke*, ed. and trans. Stephen Mitchell (New York: Vintage Books, 1984), 61.

11. Annie Dillard, *The Writing Life* (New York: Harper & Row, 1989), 68.

12. Walt Whitman, "Song of Myself," in *The American Tradition in Literature*, ed. Sculley Bradley, Richmond Croom Beatty, and E. Hudson Long (New York: W. W. Norton, 1967), 2:89.

PART I

SETTING THE STAGE

1

THE HISTORICAL JESUS

"WILL THE REAL JESUS PLEASE STAND UP?"

In *To Tell the Truth*, a long-running TV game show that began in the 1950s, three contestants all claimed to be a person described as having an unusual occupation or experience—the mystery guest. After the host read a brief biographical statement written by the mystery guest, the panelists asked questions of each contestant. The two impostors were permitted to lie, but the mystery guest was obligated to tell the truth. When the questioning was finished, each panelist voted for the person he or she thought to be the real mystery guest. Then the host said, "Will the real John/Jane X please stand up?" There was a moment of suspense. Sometimes one or two contestants began to stand, but then sat back down. Finally, the real mystery guest stood up.

Scholars have been engaged in what we now call the "quest for the historical Jesus" for more than two hundred years. Countless books have been written and debates held, and still we are asking, "Will the real Jesus please stand up?"

In reality, the debate is two thousand years old. The apostle Paul, writing twenty-some years after Jesus' death, spoke of the *hyperlian apostoloi*, the super-apostles, and the *pseudapostoloi*, the false apostles, who had come into Corinth preaching "another Jesus" and "a different gospel" (2 Corinthians 11:1-15).

We are after the real Jesus in all the meanings of the word *real*: a historically accurate picture of Jesus that captures the essence of who he was, his character and his mission.

THE HISTORICAL JESUS AND OUTSIDE EVIDENCE

The scholars' quest for the historical Jesus began after the Enlightenment when all ancient documents were beginning to be examined for their historical accuracy. We all want to know "what really happened," but that is a trickier question than we at first assume. As the novelist L. P. Hartley wrote in *The Go-Between*, "The past is a foreign country: they do things differently there."[1]

So we must explore what we mean by *history* and *historical*. Is history, to use the words of New Testament scholar, Sandra Schneiders, "What took place exactly as it took place?"[2] Her answer: "History is not a record of 'what actually happened.' It is a written re-presentation or construction of that part of 'what happened' to which the historian has access."[3] That is a properly modest estimate.

With this in mind, let's examine the extrabiblical references to Jesus—"outsider evidence," if you will. Such is important in the face of the arguments of "mythicists" who charge that Jesus was a figure who was created in order to make historical what were circulating myths at the time. Bart Ehrman, raised a fervent evangelical, now an agnostic historian of early Christian history, has taken on the growing tide of mythicists in his recent book *Did Jesus Exist? The Historical Argument for Jesus of Nazareth*.[4] So we proceed.

Pliny the Younger (16–112 CE), governor of the Roman province of Bithynia-Pontus in Asia Minor, wrote a letter to Trajan, the Roman emperor, about a secret illegal group meeting in his province. Freedom of assembly was forbidden. Pliny described the group as being of mixed socioeconomic status whose members met for common meals and sang "hymns to Christ as to a god" (*Letters* 10.96).

In the early second century, the Roman biographer Suetonius, famous for his *Lives of the Twelve Caesars*, mentions in his biography of Claudius that all Jews had been deported from Rome because of riots between Jews and Christians "at the instigation of Chrestus" (*Claudius* 25).

The Roman historian Tacitus (early second century CE) wrote in his *Annals* about Nero, who set fire to Rome and blamed the Christians. Tacitus defended the Christians as falsely accused and wrote, "Chrestus, from whom the name had its origin, suffered the extreme penalty during the reign of Tiberius at the hands of one of our procurators, Pontius Pilate, and a deadly superstition, thus checked for a moment, again broke out, not only in Judea, but also in the city" (*Annals* 15.44.2-8).

Josephus, the famous Jewish historian of the first century, referred to Jesus twice in his *Jewish Antiquities*. In one place he wrote of the execution of a man named James whom he identified as "the brother of Jesus who is called the Christ" (*Jewish Antiquities* 20.200). In a longer passage Josephus described Jesus himself:

> At this time there appeared Jesus, a wise man. . . . He was a doer of startling deeds, a teacher of people who received the truth with pleasure. And he gained a following both among many Jews and among many of Greek origin. . . . And when Pilate, because of an accusation made by the leading men among us, condemned him to the cross, those who had loved him previously did not cease to do so. . . . And up until this very day the tribe of Christians, named after him, has not died out. (*Jewish Antiquities* 18.63-64)

Lucian of Samosata (120–180 CE) wrote a satire that included references to Jesus as a "crucified sophist" whom Christians "still worship, the man crucified in Palestine because he introduced this new cult into the world" (*The Passing of Peregrinus* 11-13).[5] These outsider sources prove that Jesus was not a made-up figure, but a historical person known outside the circle of believers.

THE GOSPELS AS SOURCES AND THE MULTITUDE OF RECONSTRUCTIONS

Now we move to the four New Testament Gospels as sources for the historical Jesus. The canonical Gospels are an inextricably woven blend of what Marcus Borg calls the "Pre-Easter Jesus" and the "Post-Easter Jesus." They collect the tellings of the story of Jesus of Nazareth by those who experienced him as the Risen and Living Christ. They are like a set of transparency maps laid one on top of the other that record at least these layers:

- actual sayings and acts of the historical Jesus;
- adaptations and expansions of these sayings and acts by followers who had since experienced him as Living Lord speaking to their communities;
- remembrances passed along in oral form (what scholars today call "oral performances");
- pamphlet-sized collections of his sayings and actions preserved as units, such as the accounts of Jesus' passion;
- glimpses of the human and flawed early Christian communities trying to make their way in the world as a new religious community, first inside Judaism, then in a painful break with Judaism;
- finally, the "Gospels," written by the four evangelists traditionally identified as Matthew, Mark, Luke, and John and their communities from 70–100 CE.

Can we separate the layers? To some degree, yes, but there is wide disagreement as to *what* degree. In all cases, what we have in the Gospels is what Roman Catholic biblical scholar James Okoye calls "the history of the memory" of those early Christian communities.[6] I like to think of these communities as those tending the memory of Jesus.

By scholars' count, we are in our "third quest" for the historical Jesus since the late eighteenth century. In the current wave of the quest (begun in the 1980s) there is a great divergence on how much we can know about the historical Jesus and who this figure was. It is such a widely divergent array of reconstructions of Jesus that John Dominic Crossan, one of the leading scholars, thinks it an embarrassment. Biblical scholars James Beilby and Paul Rhodes Eddy summarize the current panoply of depictions:

> an eschatological prophet, a Galilean holy man, an occultic magician, an innovative rabbi, a trance-inducing psychotherapist, a Jewish sage, a political revolutionary, an Essene conspirator, an itinerant exorcist, an historized myth, a protoliberation theologian, a peasant artisan, a Torah-observant Pharisee, a cynic-like philosopher, a self-conscious eschatological prophet, a socioeconomic reformer, a paradoxical Messianic claimant and, finally as one who saw himself as, in some sense, the very embodiment of Yahweh-God.[7]

"Help!" we might cry. "Will the real Jesus please stand up?" Certainly in these descriptive phrases we have the language of the "experts," what amounts to scholarly shorthand. But the disagreements *are* substantial. Are the scholars like the proverbial blind men, each taking hold of a part of an elephant and claiming what they hold is the whole of it? The caution of George Tyrrell early in the twentieth century still applies; to paraphrase: as we gaze into the deep well of history to find Jesus, there is always the hazard of seeing one's own reflection at the bottom of the well and mistaking that for Jesus.[8]

Scholars in good faith disagree. There can be theological reasons for such a variety of reconstructions. If Jesus is the human prism of God's pure light, some will see the red of justice, others the orange of compassion, the yellow of joy, the green of abundant life, the blue of mystical union, the indigo of peace, the violet of sacred love.

Moreover, if Jesus is the human revelation of the divine, he will offer a God both revealed and hidden, knowable and unknowable. The quest for the historical Jesus will never end. And so, I add my small light to the ongoing quest.

MY OWN MODEL FOR THE SEARCH OF WHO JESUS WAS AND IS

My own quest for who Jesus was and is can be depicted as a Venn diagram with four interpenetrating circles. They overlap and are distinct.

FIGURE 1.

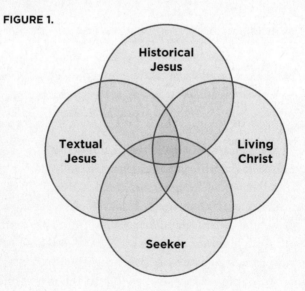

CIRCLE ONE

The first circle is the "historical Jesus." It is the reconstruction of that part of "what happened" to which the historian has access (Schneiders). We aim for what John P. Meier calls "a reliable sketch."[9] A reliable sketch with which most scholars could agree would look something like this:

- Jesus was born a Galilean Jew around 4 BCE, just before the death of Herod the Great.
- He was raised in a peasant village that, along with the whole Jewish homeland, was under the rule of the Roman Empire.
- He probably had brothers and sisters. According to the Gospels, he was a *tekton* (Mark 6:3) and the son of a *tekton* (Matthew 13:55), normally translated as "carpenter," though the word could apply to any skilled worker's trade.
- His ministry began in the late 20s CE with his baptism by John the Baptizer. It lasted between eighteen months and three years, mostly in Galilee, but may have included some trips to Jerusalem for feast days before his final trip to Jerusalem.
- He attracted a growing crowd of followers and aroused mounting opposition.
- His principal message and mission concerned the "kingdom of God," which he believed was drawing decisively and graciously near. He invited people to enter it and receive it.
- He was a healer and exorcist who brought healing of body, mind, and spirit to all without regard to social, religious, or moral standing. These miracles were witnessed by friend and foe alike, friends attributing the miracles to the power of God flowing through Jesus, foes attributing them to the power of Satan.

- He was a teacher whose most distinctive form of teaching was aphorisms, or short vivid sayings, the poetic speech of Hebrew prophets,[10] and parables, arresting and evocative stories that in their metaphorical power helped listeners to imagine what the kingdom of God was like and how their lives might be part of it.
- He befriended sinners and outcasts, eating and drinking with them as a sign of the kingdom's welcome and forgiveness. Some of them, he said, will enter the kingdom ahead of the righteous.
- He included women in his closest circle of followers and welcomed children as receivers of the kingdom of God. He was, in the estimate of novelist Mary Gordon, unique in ancient literature as "an affectionate hero."[11]
- He was a prophet who denounced the economic, political, and social injustices of the "present evil age" and prophesied the destruction of the Jewish temple.
- He entered Jerusalem before the Passover around 28–30 CE. He entered the city on a donkey as a prophetic sign that he was coming as a king. He went into the temple and overturned the tables of the money changers (for more on this Jesus story, see chapter 22). He spoke again about the destruction of the temple. These actions and words escalated the opposition to him and led the religious and political elite, afraid of an uprising against Rome, to conspire to put him to death. (Although Jesus taught nonviolence and the love of enemy, his opponents were gripped with paranoia about what might happen at Passover, that incendiary feast day when the Jews remembered their rescue from Pharaoh in Egypt.)
- Pilate sentenced him to death as a would-be "king of the Jews,"[12] a death by crucifixion, which was reserved for the worst offenders against the state.

CIRCLE TWO

The second circle is the "Living Christ." On the Sunday after Jesus' death, his followers discovered that the tomb in which his body had been placed was empty. Then the risen and living Christ began to "appear" to his disciples in what the apostle Paul described as a "spiritual body," a phrase that sought to describe the indescribable: a new kind of body, not a resuscitated corpse, but one not bound by space and time. He came to his followers, many of whom had deserted him, to forgive and call them anew to carry on his mission: "Peace to you. As the Father has sent me, so send I you" (John 20:21).

Here is the "more-than-historical Jesus," alive in the Spirit of God to those first followers and to followers ever since, still speaking, empowering, healing, and making people whole. The Gospels are shot through with resurrection light.

CIRCLE THREE

The third circle is what Sandra Schneiders calls the "textual Jesus,"[13] the Jesus known in the biblical texts that were created in what she calls "the constructive imagination." Most of us meet Jesus first of all in the biblical texts.

As we engage the texts, body, mind, and spirit are involved. Our imaginative mind is set in motion, the deep mind that apprehends deep reality. It takes what is perceived and experienced and organizes it into some new whole. To use the mystics' language: the mind descends into the heart.[14] What we encounter in the textual Jesus is not only history, but also story, poetry, myth, and symbol, what Huston Smith is attributed with calling "the technical language of religion," religion's native tongue.

The imaginative world of the Gospel writers and their communities merged the historical Jesus and the more-than-historical Jesus. And they invite our imaginative minds to enter into conversation with the texts, what might be called a "fusion of horizons." From this fusion of horizons, the creative mind creates imaginative responses that become new texts that inspire new meetings with Christ. We have been bequeathed two thousand years of stories, songs, and poetry that invite us into holy encounters with Christ.

One thinks of classical artists such as Rembrandt and Michelangelo as well as contemporary interpreters such as He Qi, Janet McKenzie, and Solomon Raj; composers such as Johann Sebastian Bach and Andrew Lloyd Weber, not to neglect the anonymous originators of the Negro spirituals; writers such as George Herbert, Phillis Wheatley, Denise Levertov, Reynolds Price, Anne Rice, captivated by the Jesus Story and turning it into art.

Texts become what Schneiders characterizes as "tents of meeting" between the divine and human, or, as Celtic Christians put it, "thin places." As we engage the biblical texts, we enter into what my teacher J. Louis Martyn called "fantastic and controlled round-table conversation." "Fantastic" refers to the imaginative knowing of the mind. "Controlled" means that we must work diligently to reconstruct history as accurately as we can; Jesus cannot be anything we want him to be. "Round-table conversation" means that we engage the text and let it engage us around a table with those who read and interpret today and with those who across two thousand years have read the text and sought to know and follow Jesus.

We might put in circle one certain deeds of Jesus, such as his baptism and death. Or vivid sayings that bear his stamp: "It is easier for a camel to go through the eye of a needle than for someone who is rich to enter the kingdom of God" (Matthew 19:24, NRSV).

We might put in circle two Jesus' appearance and words to Mary Magdalene and the others who had fled the open tomb: "Do not be afraid; go and tell my brothers to go to Galilee; there they will see me" (Matthew 28:10, NRSV).

We might put in circle three the intricately woven encounter between Jesus and the Samaritan woman in John's Gospel (John 4:4-30). This compelling narrative puts into literary form a historical encounter that also consists of layers of the history of the Johannine community between the time of Jesus to around 95 CE.

CIRCLE FOUR

The fourth circle is what I call the "seeker" circle. This circle represents you and me in our quest for who Jesus was and is. It includes "believing" seekers and nonbelieving seekers, agnostics (literally, those who don't know), all who are intrigued by the figure of Jesus. And it includes those who are some mix of faith and doubt. As Frederick Buechner wrote, "If there were no room for doubt, there would be no room for me.[15] The figure of Jesus attracts people all along the spectrum of belief and commitment.

Sandra Schneiders says the mysterious unnamed "other disciple" in John's Gospel functions as an empty set, to use a mathematical term, or empty space that the reader can enter and become "the one whom Jesus loved" (John 20:2, NRSV).[16] This is essentially the invitation of the fourth circle.

THE QUESTION AND THE QUEST

We return to the original question: How do we know the "real Jesus"? The quest will never end. However, New Testament scholar Luke Timothy Johnson asserts that we know the real Jesus not by historical examination alone, but "through practices of the faith in church, through prayer, worship, the reading of scripture and encounters with saints and strangers."[17]

Are these all the ways we can know the "real Jesus"? No, but they are a good start. Sometimes the more-than-historical Jesus comes in surprising ways no one could predict, to the outsider as well as insider. The one who "walked for us . . . on true ground"[18] is walking still, finding doors, changing lives. To this Jesus we now turn.

NOTES

1. L. P. Hartley, *The Go-Between* (1953; repr., New York: New York Review of Books, 2002), 17.

2. Sandra M. Schneiders, *The Revelatory Text: Interpreting the New Testament as Sacred Scripture*, 2nd ed. (Collegeville, MN: Liturgical Press, 1999), xxiii.

3. Ibid., xxv.

4. Bart D. Ehrman, *Did Jesus Exist? The Historical Argument for Jesus of Nazareth* (New York: HarperOne, 2012).

5. In addition to Ehrman's treatment of these sources, see Luke Timothy Johnson, *The Real Jesus: The Misguided Quest for the Historical Jesus and the Truth of the Traditional Gospels* (San Francisco: HarperSanFrancisco, 1996), 112–17.

6. James Okoye, in conversation at the Collegeville Institute, Collegeville, MN.

7. James Beilby and Paul Rhodes Eddy, eds., *The Historical Jesus: Five Views* (London: SPCK, 2010), 53.

8. George Tyrrell, *Christianity at the Crossroads* (London: Longmans, Green, 1913), 44.

9. John P. Meier, *A Marginal Jew: Rethinking the Historical Jesus*, vol. 1, *The Roots of the Problem and the Person* (New York: Doubleday, 1990).

10. See Willis Barnstone, trans., *The Poems of Jesus* (New York: W. W. Norton, 2012).

11. Mary Gordon, "The Gospel according to Mark," in *Incarnation: Contemporary Writers on the New Testament*, ed. Alfred Cord (New York: Viking, 1990), 19.

12. See Paula Fredriksen, *Jesus of Nazareth, King of the Jews: A Jewish Life and the Emergence of Christianity* (New York: Knopf, 1999).

13. Schneiders, *The Revelatory Text*, 151.

14. I am indebted to Christopher Pramuk for his incisive treatment of the role of the imaginative mind in his book on Thomas Merton: *Sophia: The Hidden Christ of Thomas Merton* (Collegeville, MN: Liturgical Press, 2009), esp. 34–35.

15. Frederick Buechner, *The Alphabet of Grace* (New York: Seabury Press, 1970), 47.

16. Sandra M. Schneiders, *Written That You May Believe: Encountering Jesus in the Fourth Gospel* (New York: Crossroad, 2003), 239.

17. Luke Timothy Johnson, "Learning the Human Jesus: Historical Criticism and Literary Criticism," in Beilby and Eddy, eds., *The Historical Jesus*, 154–55. Beilby and Eddy's book is, in my view, the best one-volume presentation of the various scholarly perspectives, from mythicist to conservative evangelical.

18. Anne Sexton, "Frenzy," in Anne Sexton, *The Complete Poems* (Boston: Houghton Mifflin, 1981), 466.

2

THE MORE-THAN-HISTORICAL JESUS

The preceding chapter considered both what we can know about the historical Jesus and the limits of what we can know. Now we turn to the more-than-historical Jesus, the Living Christ present to us and the world in the Spirit of God. The nineteenth-century English poet and Jesuit priest Gerard Manley Hopkins wrote,

> For Christ plays in ten thousand places,
> Lovely in limbs and lovely in eyes not his
> . . . through the features of men's faces.[1]

Christ is present in the loveliness of others, the compassion of others, the "justice-ing" of others, and where two or three are gathered in his name.

Christ is present in creation itself where a creation-mysticism and a Christ-mysticism merge. And Christ is present in the inner sanctuary of the self, where the Living Christ is present to us as the Beloved, speaking into our lives the grace and truth of God.

JESUS WHO LIVES IN US

The apostle Paul, with all his ferocious weaknesses and prodigious strengths, was intoxicated by Christ. His newfound faith begun on the road to Damascus en route to kill Christians was a Christ-mysticism. As one ravished by God, Paul wrote, "It is not I who live, but Christ who lives in me" (Galatians 2:20).

He took the historical Jesus seriously and sought to conform his life to that of Jesus, his teachings and his life given for us. Paul used the historical Jesus as a control to combat those who preached a "different gospel" and "another Jesus." But what was most important to him was the post-Easter Jesus, the more-than-historical Jesus: "Even though we once knew Jesus from a human point of view [literally, "according to the flesh"], we know him no longer in that way" (2 Corinthians 5:16, NRSV).

The resurrection has changed the way we look at Jesus, *and* at others. Paul now looked at Jesus from the vantage point of Easter, in light of what he called the "new creation," God's rectifying and healing power breaking into our lives and the life of the world, what Jesus called "the kingdom of God."

Transformation is at work, the change Christ would work in us: "And we all . . . beholding the glory of the Lord, are being changed into his likeness from one degree of glory to another" (2 Corinthians 3:18). In the mystery of the resurrection and the presence of the Spirit we can experience the living Christ in us, among us, between us, in our midst—as Jesus spoke of the kingdom of God as being *entos* us (Luke 17:20)—in us, among us, between us, in our midst.

In the first ending of John's Gospel, the writer says that Jesus did "many other signs" not written in the book. Yes, we say. But the second ending goes further: "But there are also many other things that Jesus did; if every one of them were written down, I suppose that the world itself could not contain the books that would be written" (John 21:25, NRSV).

We are writing still. The deeds and words of Jesus have continued in the experience of the more-than-historical Jesus, and indeed the libraries of the world cannot contain them all.

JESUS IN THE LIVES OF SEEKERS AND BELIEVERS

Jesus came to St. Francis in "one of the least of these," a leper on the streets of Rome. Francis's initial revulsion turned to compassion. He kissed the leper and encountered the Living Christ. Francis, the wealthy son of a merchant and a young soldier all too eager to go to war, became a follower of Jesus in joyful poverty and led a new movement of Jesus followers.

Christ came to Toyohiko Kagawa, the illegitimate, half-blind, sickly Japanese orphan who became the heroic slum reformer of Japan. It happened one day as he prayed, "O God, make me like Christ." A dangerous prayer.

The living Christ came to Simone Weil while she was convalescing in a monastery in Spain. Growing up in an agnostic Jewish home in France, she always had a keen sensitivity to the suffering. She joined the Socialist Worker Movement, then fell ill and went to the monastery to rest and recover. One day while reciting George Herbert's poem "Love Bade Me Welcome," her recitation took on, in her words, "the virtue of a prayer," and "Christ himself came down and took possession of me."[2] She became one of the most profound spiritual writers of the twentieth century.

Christ came to Sojourner Truth, an emancipated slave in pre–Civil War days, and empowered her to become a champion for the abolition of slavery and for the rights of women. Christ came in a vision. She said to him, "I know and don't know you . . . You seem perfectly familiar; I feel that you not only love me, but that you have always loved me."[3]

He came to Dorothy Day at the birth of her daughter Tamar in the midst of a troubled common-law marriage and led her to begin the Catholic Worker Movement on behalf of the poor of New York City and beyond.

Christ came to a West Coast novelist, Anne Lamott, in a quite unexpected way. Her career had gotten off to a good start, but her life careened this way and that. She had always had a spiritual side, but this Jesus business was for the birds. Then, somehow she found God (or God found her) in a little ghetto church in Marin County across from a flea market: "It is where I was taken in when I had nothing to give," she writes, "and it has become in the truest, deepest sense, my home. My home-base."[4] She writes:

> I did not mean to be a Christian. . . . My first words upon encountering the presence of Jesus for the first time 12 years ago were, "I would rather die." I really would rather have died at that point than to have my wonderful brilliant left-wing non-believer friends know that I had begun to love Jesus. I think they would have been less appalled if I had developed a close personal friendship with Strom Thurmond.[5]

The encounter with Jesus took place in her houseboat, where she was just home recovering from an abortion. She was weak from loss of blood and in a kind of haze produced by a combination of pain medication and whiskey. She suddenly sensed Jesus' presence in the room, sitting in the corner of the room "watching me with patience and love"; she turned away from him to the wall and said out loud, "I would rather die."[6] She fell asleep, and in the morning he was gone.

The next day she wondered whether it had been a hallucination "born of fear and self-loathing and booze and loss of blood."[7] This Jesus, she says, was relentless: "I didn't experience him so much as the hound of heaven, as the old description has it, as the alley cat of heaven, who seemed to believe that if it just keeps showing up, mewling outside your door, you'd eventually open up and give him a bowl of milk."[8]

Lamott resisted until a week or so later when she returned to her church, which had become God's salvation to her. She writes, "That's where I was when I came to. And then I came to believe."[9] In church that day, the sermon seemed to her about as sensible as someone trying to convince her of "the existence of extraterrestrials." But the last song in the worship service did it:

> The last song was so deep and raw and pure that I could not escape. It was as if the people were singing in between the notes, weeping and joyful at the same time, and I felt like their voices or *something* was rocking me in its bosom, holding me like a scared kid, and I opened up to that feeling—and it washed over me.[10]

She began to cry and left before the benediction. As she raced home, she felt Christ, like a little cat, running along at her heels. When she arrived at her houseboat, she paused, opened the door and said to Christ, "F--- it: I quit. . . . All right. You can come in." This, she says, "was my beautiful moment of conversion."[11]

I close with one more Jesus story, that of Albert Schweitzer. A student of the great French organist and composer Charles-Marie Widor, before the age of thirty Schweitzer had become a Bach scholar and an accomplished organist in his own right. He was at the same time a brilliant theologian and biblical scholar.

In his monumental *Quest of the Historical Jesus* (first published in 1906), Schweitzer sought to use all the best historical tools to recover the historical Jesus. He studied all the scholars who had sought to reconstruct Jesus' life. He concluded that they had created their Jesus in the image of nineteenth-century liberalism rather than revealing the historical Jesus.

His own best reconstruction of Jesus' life determined that Jesus was an apocalyptic prophet who thought that his death would usher in the final kingdom of God and died a mistaken man, in that the final, completed kingdom did not come as he had hoped. Schweitzer knew that his historical conclusions—that Jesus could have been wrong—would shake most Christians, but for him it was a new door. He would concentrate on the moral and spiritual teachings of Jesus, on Jesus' spiritual impact on him now. We had, he said, tried to force Jesus into our time: "But he does not stay; he passes by our time and returns to his own."[12]

Schweitzer wrote in the conclusion of his book, "But the truth is, it is not Jesus as historically known, but Jesus as spiritually arisen with men, who is significant for our own time and can help it."[13]

And then there is the very last paragraph of the volume, luminous words that I met first in the form of an anthem. They go where his scholarship could not lead him:

> He comes to us as One unknown, without a name, as of old, by the lake-side, He came to those men who knew Him not. He speaks to us the same word: "Follow thou me!" and sets us to the tasks which He has to fulfill for our time. He commands. And to those who obey Him, whether they be wise or simple, He will reveal Himself in the toils, the conflicts, the sufferings which they shall pass through in His fellowship, and, as an ineffable mystery, they shall learn in their own experience Who He is.[14]

The passage was prescient of what was to come. Schweitzer decided to enter medical school so that he could go to Africa and found a hospital. His friends thought he was crazy and needed to reconsider his choice. Widor, who loved him like a son, said he should not go. Schweitzer commented that earlier in his life he would have given the same advice. But he had heard the call, and he went. He wrote, "I wanted to be a doctor that I might be able to work without having to talk." "For years," he said, "I had been giving myself out in words." Now he would be putting the "religion of love" actually into practice.[15]

His following of Jesus led him to found the hospital in Lambaréné. He was approved by the Paris Missionary Society to go as a doctor only if he promised not to confuse the missionaries and Africans with his heretical teaching and preaching! His theology might have been considered heresy, but his life was conformed to the way of Jesus the Christ.

When Schweitzer was given the Nobel Prize, someone said, "I'd like to be Albert Schweitzer if only I could commute!" Christ won't let us commute. His call involves the whole of us, or as much of the whole of us as we are able to give at the time. We start where we are, not where we aren't; then, who knows what the historical and more-than-historical Jesus will do in us, through us?

NOTES

1. Gerard Manley Hopkins, "As kingfishers catch fire, dragonflies draw flame," in Gerard Manley Hopkins, *Poems and Prose of Gerard Manley Hopkins* (New York: Penguin Books, 1985), 51.

2. Simone Weil, *The Simone Weil Reader*, ed. George A. Panichas (New York: D. McKay, 1977), 16.

3. Olive Gilbert, *Narrative of Sojourner Truth* (New York: Arno Press, 1968), 67–69.

4. Anne Lamott, "Word by Word: Spiritual Chemotherapy," February 13, 1997, http://www.salon.com/1997/02/13/lamott970213/.

5. Ibid.

6. Anne Lamott, *Traveling Mercies: Some Thoughts on Faith* (New York: Random House, 1999), 49.

7. Ibid., 50.

8. Lamott, "Word by Word."

9. Ibid.

10. Lamott, *Traveling Mercies*, 50.

11. Ibid.

12. Albert Schweitzer, *The Quest of the Historical Jesus: A Critical Study of Its Progress from Reimarus to Wrede* (Baltimore: Johns Hopkins University Press, with the Albert Schweitzer Institute, 1998), 399.

13. Ibid., 401.

14. Ibid., 403.

15. Albert Schweitzer, *Out of My Life and Thought: An Autobiography*, trans. C. T. Campion (New York: Holt, 1933), 114–15.

PART II
THE BEGINNINGS

3

THE BEGINNINGS OF THE JESUS STORY

Where does the Jesus Story begin? Most historians begin with Jesus' baptism, where Mark's Gospel begins. But each of the four canonical Gospels gives a different answer to the question.

The coming of Jesus brought into being a new literary form to tell his life, "a new utterance" called "gospel."[1] The word *gospel* (*euangelion* in Greek) literally means "good news." Each of the Gospel writers shared the good news of their Jesus Story in different ways.

Mark, the earliest of the biblical Gospels, plunged in at the Jordan River, where Jesus was baptized by John the Baptizer. Novelist Reynolds Price calls the author of Mark "the most original narrative writer in history."[2] Mark's story of Jesus became the template for Matthew and Luke, the three of which are known as the Synoptic Gospels.

"The beginning of the gospel of Jesus Christ the Son of God" is how Mark begins. Then nine verses down, Jesus is baptized. When he came up out of the water, the heavens were "torn open," the Spirit of God descended like a dove, and a voice came from heaven saying, "You are my Son, the Beloved; with you I am well pleased" (Mark 1:11, NRSV).

Did Jesus *feel* God's pleasure at that moment? Was it the first time he felt the pleasure of God?

Mark's vision is that Jesus was God's son adopted at baptism and called to God's mission in the world. Isaiah 61 describes what the vocation of such a Spirit-filled son would be about: good news to the poor, care of the brokenhearted, liberty to captives, blind eyes opened, and prison doors flung wide. Jesus would use this text in his inaugural sermon in his hometown, Nazareth. The results were not immediately encouraging. His audience hauled him out of the synagogue and tried to throw him off a cliff (Luke 4:16-30).

Matthew's Gospel begins, "The book of the genesis of Jesus, son of David, son of Abraham." The writer (traditionally identified as the apostle Matthew) plants Jesus deeply in the history and life of the Jewish people. Immediately he traces Jesus' genealogy from Abraham to Joseph, husband of Mary—forty-two generations.

The fact that Jesus came from Abraham's family tree meant that Jesus was a bona fide Jew, and as Howard Thurman wrote, "The miracle of the Jewish people is almost as breathtaking as the miracle of Jesus."[3]

Enter Joseph, betrothed in marriage to Mary. He had just discovered that Mary was with child. He knew he was not the father; the only conclusion he could imagine was that she had been with another man. His options were two. The first was to expose her publically for the presumed sin of adultery, which at best would mean her disgrace and banishment, and at worst would mean death by stoning for her and her unborn child. The second option was to divorce her quietly and get on with his suddenly altered life as best he could. Joseph, being a "just man," a *tsaddiq* in Hebrew tradition, a man both righteous and merciful, resolved to pursue option two.

But God had other plans, option three. God intervened by way of the visitation of an angel in a dream. (The word *angel* in the Bible means "messenger," specifically "messenger of God.") The angel said, "Joseph, son of David, do not be afraid to take Mary as your wife, for the child conceived in her is from the Holy Spirit" (Matthew 1:20, NRSV). Then the Gospel writer quotes Hebrew Scripture, which was his modus operandi, seeing Jesus' life and all life as a fulfillment of Scripture and the promises of God: "Behold, a virgin shall conceive and bear a son, and his name shall be called Emmanuel (which means, God with us)" (Matthew 1:23).

When Joseph awoke from the dream, he did as the angel commanded—a decision requiring no little courage. He took Mary as his wife, to love, honor, and cherish her—and to love, honor, and cherish her child as well.

The Fourth Gospel, attributed traditionally to John, son of Zebedee, traces the life story of Jesus all the way back to the beginning of creation:

> In the beginning was the Word, and the Word was with God, and the Word was God. . . . And the Word became flesh and dwelt among us. (John 1:1,14)

The Greek word for "Word" is *logos*, but here is a more Hebraic way of translating the text:

> In the beginning was the Speaking,
> and the Speaking was with God,
> and the Speaking was God. . . .
> And the Speaking became flesh and tabernacled with us.

Later Hebrew Scripture would describe this Speaking *of* God *with* God at the beginning as the *Hokmah* of God, the Wisdom of God, personified as the daughter of God dancing in God's presence and being cocreator of the world with God (see Proverbs 8:22-31). So one way to understand Jesus is as the eternal wisdom of God who has entered our human, historical sphere. *Hokmah*, Daughter Wisdom, has become the Beloved Son.

John begins his Gospel with this poem, a "theopoetic"[4] that, as Amos Wilder has said, is the womb of all theology. John's way of imagining the beginning of Jesus as the eternal Word made flesh will open to us the idea of the Christ presence as the divine presence of God throughout all history and in all religions, God seeking us through the Christ forever.

Luke's account of the Jesus story begins with a salutation, "Dear Theophilus," a document written to a Greek-speaking audience. Luke's expressed purpose was to write "an orderly account" of the stories and sayings of Jesus that had been passed down to him (Luke 1:1-4).

He launches his Gospel, not at the river Jordan, not in Abrahamic lineage with Joseph as the hero, not at creation's beginning, but on the stage of world history: "In the days of Herod, king of Judea" (Luke 1:5); and a few verses down, "In those days a decree went out from Caesar Augustus that all the world should be taxed" (Luke 2:1).

The hero of Luke's story about Jesus' beginning is not Joseph, but Mary, and his account is like a Broadway musical with characters suddenly bursting into song. Think of Luke as Stephen Sondheim. Jesus' conception and birth began at the invitation of an angel to a teenaged Jewish girl. The scene is often called the "Annunciation" or "Announcement," which has been famously captured numerous times in Western art. I prefer to name it the "Call of Mary" because it resembles the call stories of many other great Hebrew figures: Abraham and Sarah, Hagar, Moses, Samuel, Isaiah, Amos, Jeremiah.

The angel appeared to Mary with this greeting: "Hail, O favored one, the Lord is with you!" (Luke 1:28). The text says that she was "greatly troubled," which probably means "shaking in her sandals." Then the angel said, "Do not be afraid, Mary, for you have found favor with God. And behold, you will conceive in your womb and bear a son, and you shall call his name Jesus" (Luke 1:30-31). (Does it sound like a chant, a recitative?) Mary replied, "How can this be, since I know not a man?" The angel, speaking the language of mystery, said:

> The Holy Spirit will come upon you,
> and the power of the Most High will overshadow you;
> therefore the child to be born will be called holy,
> the Son of God. (Luke 1:35)

Then Mary said yes. She offered no arguments, showed no hesitation—unlike the responses in many of the other call stories in Scripture—but spoke only these simple words: "Here I am, the servant of the Lord. Let it be to me according to your word" (see Luke 1:38).

Perhaps the call and Mary's response are best captured in poetry. Poetry slows us down, creates silences, settles us with music, helps us ponder the mingling of the divine and the human in our lives. Poet Denise Levertov has captured the call of Mary in her poem "Annunciation":

> . . . we are told of meek obedience. No one mentions
> courage.
> The engendering Spirit
> did not enter her without consent.
> God waited.
> She was free
> to accept or to refuse, choice
> integral to humanness. . . .

> Called to a destiny more momentous
> than any in all of time,
> she did not quail,
> only asked
> a simple, "How can this be?"
> and gravely, courteously,
> took to heart the angel's reply,

perceiving instantly
the astounding ministry she was offered:

to bear in her womb
infinite weight and lightness; to carry
in hidden, finite inwardness,
nine months of Eternity; to contain
in slender vase of being,
the sum of power—
in narrow flesh,
the sum of light.
Then bring to birth,
push out into air, a Man-child
needing, like any other
milk and love—
but who was God. . . .

She did not cry, "I cannot, I am not worthy,"
nor, "I have not the strength."
She did not submit with gritted teeth,
raging, coerced,
bravest of all humans, consent illumined her. . . .
Consent,
courage unparalleled
opened her utterly.[5]

Thus, in Luke's Gospel, Jesus' story begins where courage and consent meet. Then Luke gives his own genealogy, which takes Jesus' family tree all the way back to Adam. Jesus will be the "savior of the world"—not Caesar, who was often given this title, but Jesus. He is the new humanity.

Here are four stories, each pondering the mystery of Jesus. They use the language of story, metaphor, myth, and poetry. How else do we describe the ineffable?

As I ponder the mystery of Jesus' humanity and divinity, I see these two kinds of Christians. First, there are those who for all the right reasons need Jesus to be *more* than they are, divine, divinely created. How else could he reveal the true God in his being? Come to save? Why else would they trust their lives to him and follow him above all others?

Then there are those who for all the right reasons need Jesus to be *exactly* who they are, as human as they, though more fully so, with the same genetic package of human capacities, the same possibility of the divine Spirit and human flesh joined. How else could they be called to follow him, imitate him, *be* him in the world? Why would they even try if they, human, had to be like Jesus, perfectly divine?

The Gospels speak to both kinds of Christians and seek to hold the mystery of Jesus as *mystery*, this one who was both "genuine humanity" and "genuine divine presence."

The stories of the beginning of Jesus go beyond gynecological fact to the mystery of God-with-us in Jesus. There is the human historical Jesus of Nazareth, but there is also "more." The Gospels probe this "more." The ancient yearnings of humankind find their fulfillment in Jesus as the incarnation of God.

The twentieth-century English poet E. H. W. Meyerstein wrote, "Myth is my tongue, which means not that I cheat, but stagger in a light too great to bear." The four Gospels stagger in this light and come forth with a "new utterance" called gospel, good news. This is how we begin the Jesus Story.

NOTES

1. Amos N. Wilder, *Early Christian Rhetoric: The Language of the Gospel* (Cambridge, MA: Harvard University Press, 1971), 1–17.

2. Reynolds Price, *The Three Gospels* (New York: Scribner, 1996), 17.

3. Howard Thurman, *Jesus and the Disinherited* (Boston: Beacon Press, 1976), 15.

4. Amos Wilder, *Theopoetic: Theology and the Religious Imagination* (Philadelphia: Fortress Press, 1976).

5. Denise Levertov, "Annunciation," in *Selected Poems* (New York: New Directions, 2002), 162–64.

4

JESUS THE BOY, THE SON, THE BELOVED

Our minds are hungry for details about Jesus' growing up years. What was he like? Did he experience a first kiss, fight with his siblings, rebel against his parents? Did he study with rabbis in Nazareth? The four canonical Gospels are silent on these years, save one tantalizing glimpse in Luke 2, the story of Jesus at age twelve on a trip with his parents to Jerusalem for Passover. It is an illuminating glimpse of a holy and human boy.

Luke's story is quite different from some of the boyhood stories in the recently discovered apocryphal Gospels at Nag Hammadi, which display Jesus as a divine child more akin to a Superboy comic strip or a character in a Stephen King novel.[1]

In the *Infancy Gospel of Thomas* (not to be confused with the *Gospel of Thomas*), we see Jesus from the ages of five to twelve. In an early story, he fashions twelve clay sparrows from mud. When he is accused of violating the Sabbath by working on them, he then magically turns them into live birds that fly away.

In another story, a young fellow bumps into the child Jesus. Jesus strikes him dead. When the boy's parents complain to Joseph and threaten to run Joseph and his family out of town, Jesus punishes them with blindness.

But as Jesus grows older, his magical powers grow more benevolent. He heals and saves the life of a boy who has cut his foot with an ax. He helps Joseph, who has cut a board the wrong length, by stretching the board to the correct measurement. In a Syriac variant on this Gospel, Jesus first ruins the cloths of a dyer in his shop, and then miraculously turns them into the colors the dyer needs.

In the *Arabic Infancy Gospel*, Jesus is pursuing some children who don't want to play with him. They hide from him. He promptly turns them into goats. The children's parents are mortified and plead with him on behalf of their children. Jesus then turns them back into children, and they play together. (I bet they did!) We can imagine the parents saying to them, "The next time Jesus wants you to play with him, just go with it!"

These stories likely make us cringe. Jesus appears to be a superhuman magician who uses his powers however he wishes—and his wishes are far from pure. His "character" is far from the Jesus we meet in the New Testament Gospels.

In marked contrast, Luke's lone Gospel account of the twelve-year-old Jesus is quite modest. Jesus' holiness is not about magical powers, but about his closeness to God and desire to do whatever pleases God.

JESUS THE BOY

Luke described how Mary and Joseph raised Jesus in an observant Jewish home, performing "everything required by the law of the Lord" (Luke 2:39, NRSV), and how Jesus "grew and became strong, filled with wisdom; and the favor of the Lord was upon him" (Luke 2:40, NRSV). One cannot ignore that Jesus came from deep Jewish roots.

Jesus grew up, and he dresses like a Jew. Specifically, he wears *tzitzit*, "fringes."[2] Observant Jewish males of Jesus' day wore fringes on their clothing to remind them of the 613 commandments. (These fringes are on the tallit, the prayer shawl still worn in Jewish worship today.) When a woman who suffered from a hemorrhage came to Jesus for healing and "touched the fringe of his garment" (Matthew 9:20), she touched the fringes worn by an observant Jew.[3] That's who Jesus was, how he was raised. Many of the most terrible of distortions of who Jesus was over the centuries have come by ignoring his Jewishness.

But the nature of his Jewish faith was reformist. He preached a deeper way to live Torah. And the way was based on his intimate relationship with Yahweh whom he called *Abba*. Such intimacy may have begun with what liberation theologian Dorothee Soelle called "childhood mysticism."[4] Luke's story gives us a clue.

Jesus and his family were on their annual pilgrimage from Nazareth to Jerusalem for Passover. It was a sixty-five mile trip each way, which took three days to travel on foot.

When the Passover festival was over, the pilgrims, including Jesus' family, packed up and began their trip home. Jesus missed the departure of the caravan.

Mary and Joseph did not miss Jesus until the group stopped for the night. It is not difficult to see how it could happen to even the most loving parents: the hubbub of more than a million pilgrims in Jerusalem, the village traveling together, Mary and Joseph assuming that Jesus was playing with his friends. The African proverb says that it takes a village to raise a child. It also takes a village to *lose* one.

When the caravan stopped for the night and Mary and Joseph could not find Jesus, we can imagine their panic. We might imagine that it was like the movie *Home Alone*, in which the family and relatives hustle off to the airport for a Christmas trip to Europe and leave the youngest son asleep in his upstairs sleeping cove. Have you ever lost a child in a crowd? Have you ever gotten lost yourself?

Mary and Joseph had to spend a restless night in worry before they could return to Jerusalem the next morning by daylight. When they got there, they searched the city to no avail. It was not until the next day (day number three) that they found him: he was in the temple, sitting with the teachers, listening, asking, and answering questions. The teachers, the text says, were "amazed" by his precocious understanding.

We love this scene—Jesus the boy in the temple. It is one of those scenes chosen to be depicted in illustrated Bibles, or hung on Sunday school walls. Pictured there is a young boy talking with the elders of his religion.

When Mary and Joseph found him, we can imagine their tumultuous jumble of emotions. Mary said, "Child, why have your treated us like this?" (Sound familiar?) Then she added, "Look, your father and I have been searching for you with great anxiety" (Luke 2:48, NRSV). Or, as we would say now, "We've been worried sick."

Jesus responded with these vivid, sharp words: "Why were you searching for me? Did you not know that I must be in my Father's house?" (Luke 2:49, NRSV).

Other translations, such as the New King James Version, read, "Did you not know I must be about my Father's business?" Both meanings—"in my Father's house" and "about my Father's business"—work. Jesus might have said, "Where else would I be but in the temple? You brought me here for dedication when I was an infant, and you have taken me here every year since. You've seen my love of this place. Where else would I be?" Or he might have asked, "You've known my desire to be about my heavenly Father's work. Where else would I be but here?"

All through this episode, Mary and Joseph are named as Jesus' "parents," but in this response, Jesus is claiming a higher loyalty and more intimate relation to his heavenly parent. In all his prayers in the Gospels (except the one on the cross, where he quoted Psalm 22), Jesus addressed God as *Abba*, the Aramaic word for "father" or "papa." His life was grounded in what we could call his "Abba-experience,"[5] a

relationship with God marked by intimacy, confidence, obedience, and trust.

Luke says that Jesus' parents did not understand what he
said, and that his mother "kept," or pondered, these things in
her heart. And the text says that Jesus returned with them to
Nazareth and was "obedient" to them. I bet he was.

GROWING UP IN NAZARETH

We have no historical record or Gospel account of what happened to Jesus between ages twelve and thirty, between the
temple incident and the baptism in the Jordan. A friend and
associate, Cheryl Patterson, suggests that this is because he
was grounded for eighteen years!

Speculations abound. Some say that Jesus studied with the
Essene community at the Dead Sea. It appears likely that his
cousin John the Baptizer did so. Some suggest that Jesus went
to India and learned wisdom from the East. But scholars' best
guess is that he stayed close to home, where he was formed by
religious training from his family and in the synagogue.

A recent archeological discovery may give us something
more to reflect upon about Jesus' growing-up years. Just four
miles northwest of Nazareth was a large cosmopolitan Roman city, Sepphoris.[6] It had been burned to ashes in 4 BCE
when a Jewish revolt, led by Judah the Galilean, provoked
Roman military response. Then Herod Antipas had it rebuilt
to new glory. In his *Jewish Antiquities,* the first-century historian Josephus called it an "ornament of all Galilee" (18.27)

During Jesus' growing-up years, a massive rebuilding of
the city was happening, including a three-thousand-seat the-
ater and a palace. The city was populated by Jews and Romans. It was on a trade route where people passed from east
to west, north to south. Were Joseph the carpenter and Jesus
his apprentice involved in any of these projects? Was Jesus
exposed to the Roman Hellenistic culture by the proximity of

Sepphoris? Scholars can answer only, "Perhaps," but it is a richly suggestive perhaps.

Biblical scholar John P. Meier suggests that Jesus was trilingual: he spoke Aramaic, read and spoke Hebrew, and knew Greek.[7] Jesus also would have observed other things in the social and political worlds of Nazareth, Sepphoris, and wider Galilee: the ruthless imperial power of Rome, the deals that Jewish leaders made with Rome to keep the "peace," and the dramatic difference between rich and poor, powerful and powerless. Hebrew prophets had also noticed such things.

When Sepphoris was destroyed by the Roman army, two thousand Jewish men were crucified along the public roads. This horror would have seared the collective memory of the Galilean people.

Jesus himself was raised in a small peasant village. Contemporary archeological excavations suggest that Nazareth was a village of about two hundred residents.[8] When Jesus was dedicated in the temple, his parents offered as a sacrifice two turtledoves, a provision made for the poor. New Testament scholar Raymond Brown suggests that Jesus' family and social/religious circle were among the *anawim*, "poor ones."[9] They were described by Luke as those "looking for the redemption of Israel" (Luke 2:38, NRSV). That is, their hope was in God and God alone to come in power, delivering Israel from Roman oppression and setting up God's reign on earth.

JESUS' BAPTISM

Mark's Gospel records that when John baptized Jesus, a voice from heaven said, "You are my Son, the Beloved; with you I am well pleased" (Mark 1:11, NRSV). When did Jesus first experience this belovedness as God's son? In his mother's arms, at Joseph's side, walking Galilean hills and flower-strewn meadows, in mystical encounters? Of course, we cannot know, but the message was made clear at his baptism.

How was the human Jesus, as a boy and as a man, also holy? His holiness was his desire to be obedient to whatever he perceived God to be asking, his desire to be a pure prism of God's holy light, a vessel of God's power and compassion. And it was based upon his intimate relationship with God, his *Abba*.

At the heart of Jesus' spirituality was his consciousness of being the beloved Son of God, his *Abba*. At the heart of our own spiritual quest is becoming who we are, the beloved of God. In his book *Life of the Beloved*, Henri Nouwen writes:

> All I want to say to you is "You are the Beloved," and all I hope is that you can hear these words as spoken to you with all the tenderness and force that love can hold. My only desire is to make these words reverberate in every corner of your being—"You are the Beloved."[10]

We move now to Jesus' baptism and the disclosure of his belovedness in God's eyes.

NOTES

1. See Wilhelm Schneemelcher, ed., *New Testament Apocrypha*, vol. 1, *Gospels and Related Writings*, rev. ed. (Louisville: Westminster John Knox Press, 2003), 444–49, 453, 461.

2. Amy-Jill Levine, *The Misunderstood Jew: The Church and the Scandal of the Jewish Jesus* (San Francisco: HarperSanFrancisco, 2006), 23.

3. See ibid., 23–24.

4. Dorothee Soelle, *The Silent Cry: Mysticism and Resistance* (Minneapolis: Fortress Press, 2001), 9–14.

5. Joachim Jeremias, *New Testament Theology: The Proclamation of Jesus* (New York: Scribner, 1971), 61ff. See also H. Stephen Shoemaker, *Finding Jesus in His Prayers* (Nashville: Abingdon Press, 2004), 36ff.

6. James F. Strange, "Sepphoris" . . . 1090–93.

7. See John P. Meier, *A Marginal Jew: Rethinking the Historical Jesus* (New York: Doubleday, 1991), 266–76.

8. John Dominic Crossan and Jonathan L. Reed, *Excavating Jesus: Beneath the Stones, Behind the Text* (San Francisco: HarperSanFrancisco, 2001), 37.

9. Raymond E. Brown, *The Birth of the Messiah: A Commentary on the Birth Narratives in the Gospels of Matthew and Luke* (New York: Doubleday, 1977), 328–65.

10. Henri J. M. Nouwen, *Life of the Beloved: Spiritual Living in a Secular World* (New York: Crossroad, 1993), 26.

5

BAPTISM AND TEMPTATION

Historians generally designate two events in the life of Jesus as the most indisputably historical: Jesus' baptism and crucifixion. So we begin here with his baptism.

THE BAPTISM

The baptizer was the one we call John the Baptist and the place was the Jordan River in the Judean wilderness. He wore animal skins and ate wild locusts, and he called the nation to repent so to escape the coming judgment of God. A one-man reform movement in first-century Judaism, John offered a way of radical repentance and purification that didn't depend on the temple sacrifice system. You could be washed for free, the only requirement being a heart ready to turn and be changed by God.

The Jewish historian of that day, Josephus, described him this way: "He was a good man and had exhorted the Jews to lead righteous lives, to practice justice toward their fellow and piety toward God, and in so doing, join in baptism" (*Jewish Antiquities* 18:117).

John was a popular prophet, which made him a threat to Herod, who later had him beheaded. That John called

Herod's marriage to his brother's wife immoral may have been the last straw. People streamed to him to be baptized. His baptism was a one-time baptism of repentance, not the daily washings practiced by the Dead Sea community, the Essenes, with whom John may have studied. He may have seen his message of repentance as the last call for the nation to repent and be saved from the coming judgment.

Jesus came for baptism in identification with his Jewish people. What happened at the baptism was a startling intervention by God. As described by Mark, the heavens were torn open, the Spirit descended as a dove, and a voice said to Jesus, "You are my Son, the beloved in whom I am well pleased, in whom I take delight." We do not know whether God's voice was heard by those around or whether Jesus had received such a message before, but the event was life-changing. Jesus was being called as the son/servant of God.

THE WILDERNESS TEMPTATIONS

What happened next was just as surprising. The same Spirit who anointed him now drove him into the wilderness to be tempted (see Mark 1:9-13). It is a shocking sequence: baptism, blessing, call, wilderness, temptation, Satan.

There were things to work out. What did it mean for Jesus to be the anointed son/servant of God? Philosopher and theologian Diogenes Allen wrote:

> We do not usually think of temptations as a place to find help. But there are some temptations which stand at the entrance. There are some temptations which even to recognize as temptations and to feel the conflict of being pulled in two directions is to have found the gateway to a new path.[1]

The temptations happened so that Jesus could discern and prove what it meant for him to be about his mission as God's son in the world.

When Muhammad received his overpowering vision from God on Mount Hira in 610 CE, which began his career as a prophet of God, he at first did not know whether the vision came from God or from a *jinn*, an evil spirit. In contrast, Jesus knew whom he was facing.

The one who confronted Jesus in Matthew, Mark, and Luke is variously described as "Satan" (Mark 1:13), "the devil" (Matthew 4:1; Luke 4:2-3), and "the tempter" (Matthew 4:3). We can see these temptations as the deepest possible conversation happening in Jesus' head. In the Hebrew, *satan* means "accuser." Jesus at one point calls Satan "the father of lies" (John 8:44). The voice of Satan was the lying, accusing, tempting voice that came to distract Jesus from his true mission as the Son of God.

Jesus was in the wilderness forty days, the period of time it took him to settle things in his mind and spirit.

THE FIRST TEMPTATION

The first temptation came when Jesus was famished from his days of fasting. The tempter said, "If you are the Son of God, command this stone to become a loaf of bread" (Luke 4:3, NRSV). Jesus answered with a quotation from Hebrew Scripture: "It is written, 'One does not live by bread alone, but by every word that comes from the mouth of God" (Matthew 4:4, NRSV).

There are several temptations inherent in this one. One is the temptation to see this life solely in terms of the material, rather than a reality composed of both the material and spiritual, indissolubly so. Matter *matters*! Otherwise, God would not have become matter in Jesus. But this is matter infused with the spirit. We are both matter and spirit, clay and spark.

Physical hunger is important to God. Jesus will feed the hungry. But his mission is more. He will provide another bread, bread for the spirit.

Here is the temptation of materialism: not just consumerism, but the temptation to define life solely in terms of the physical, the material. Jesus once said, "My food is to do the will of him who sent me" (John 4:34).

It is also the temptation to the miraculous. "Here, Jesus," says the tempter, "be a magician. You're hungry. Turn this stone into bread." But the God of Jesus is not that kind of God, and Jesus will not be that kind of Son of God. Jesus did not need to be miraculous to prove who he was. In fact, John's Gospel reports that Jesus "did not entrust himself" to those who believed in him only because of the signs (miracles) he performed (John 2:23-24).

THE SECOND TEMPTATION

The second temptation (in Luke's order) happened like this: The devil swooped Jesus up to a place where he could see all the kingdoms of the world. Matthew locates the event on "a very high mountain," but it was higher than any geographical point. It was a place in Jesus' mind's eye where he could see *all* the kingdoms of the world: Jerusalem, Rome, Babylon, Egypt, Persia, India.

The devil said, "To you I will give all this authority and their glory; for it has been delivered to me, and I will give it to whom I will. If you, then, will worship me, it shall all be yours" (Luke 4:6-7).

The second temptation is to power and glory, *political* power and glory. Would Jesus be a political Messiah and deliver Israel from Rome? Would he be a Caesar and set up a true *Pax Romana*? Would he use the power of the sword to advance his spiritual goals? Would he be about violent justice or nonviolent justice? Would he use coercive power to advance the kingdom of God on earth? Or would he be a different kind of son/servant/king?

Jesus answered the second temptation, again, with words from Hebrew Scripture: "It is written, 'Worship the Lord your God, and serve only him'" (Luke 4:8, NRSV).

In Russian novelist Fyodor Dostoevsky's *The Brothers Karamazov*, we find the famous parable of the "Grand

Inquisitor." In it, Jesus comes to Seville, Spain, during the Spanish Inquisition, where the church and state have joined arms to find and kill all heretics as well as to expel all Jews from Spain. Jesus has come to comfort the persecuted and fearful masses. The head of the Inquisition sees Jesus and summons him for interrogation.

He tells Jesus that Jesus made all the wrong choices in the wilderness temptations, that he was offered the three great powers of miracle, mystery, and authority, but he turned them down for the sake of human freedom. Jesus wanted us to come to God only in freedom and love. The Inquisitor tells Jesus that Jesus chose everything "unusual, enigmatic and indefinite."[2]

The Grand Inquisitor says that he has corrected Jesus' mistakes. People are too weak and stupid to choose what is right. So now the church and state have joined to command the powers of miracle, mystery, and authority. "Why have you come to interfere?" the Inquisitor asks.

Jesus never says a word during the entire interrogation. It has become a soliloquy. The Inquisitor, who had planned to burn Jesus at the stake, decides to release him. Jesus' only answer? He kisses the Grand Inquisitor on the lips and slips silently out into the night.

THE THIRD TEMPTATION

In the third temptation, the devil took Jesus to the pinnacle of the temple in Jerusalem and said, "If you are the Son of God, throw yourself down from here, for it is written, [Now the *devil* quotes Scripture!] 'God will give his angels charge of you, to guard you,' and 'On their hands they will bear you up, lest you strike your foot against a stone'" (Luke 4:10-11, adapted).

The devil here quoted from a beloved psalm, Psalm 91:11-12, a psalm speaking of our deep trust in God. Satan is using Scripture to tempt Jesus. As Shakespeare observed in *The Merchant of Venice*, "The devil can cite scripture for his purpose."

What was the temptation? It is subtle and reaches to the depth of our hearts. We could call it the temptation to security and magical thinking. It is the temptation to live under the illusion that we can control all things. Who does not wish such, especially in face of the suffering of the innocent and the young?

The devil quotes a psalm that probes our most fervent trust in God to care for us and to protect us from harm. So we might say, "I trust God to care for me, to be always with me, but can God protect me from physical and emotional harm? Will God spare me from tragedy? Spare my children?"

The temptation to magical thinking goes something like this: "If I'm good enough, faithful enough, if I love God enough, I will be spared injury, illness, tragedy, and untimely death." The devil says to Jesus, "If you're the Son of God, jump off the temple ledge, and the angels will parachute you to the ground. God will protect you; God will protect *you*!"

The other dimension in the temptation is to choose security over our mission in life. Will Jesus stay true to his mission in life without magical thinking, instead trusting God utterly with his life and death? Will *we*? No guarantees included?

Jesus could have fled in his final hour, slipped off to France with Mary Magdalene, raised a family, and died a natural death. Some think this is what happened. And Nikos Kazantzakis, in his novel *The Last Temptation of Christ*, suggests that this was Jesus' last temptation—which Jesus ultimately refused. But Jesus would stay true to his mission no matter what! To flee would undermine the mission of the kingdom of God that he preached.

Jesus answers the tempter's use of Scripture with one last quotation from the Hebrew Scripture: "It is said, 'Do not put the Lord your God to the test'" (Luke 4:12, NRSV).

Here is the end of magical thinking, the end of bargaining. It is abandonment to divine providence, to the eternal love of God, who, we trust, is redeeming all things, all living, all loss, all grieving, working with us so that all accidents of fate, chance, genetics, injury, and illness are gathered into God's purpose.

ONGOING TEMPTATIONS

In Luke's Gospel, the last sentence of the temptation narrative foreshadows what is to come and tells honest truth that the most crucial temptations come and come again: "And when the devil had ended every temptation, he departed from him *until an opportune time*" (Luke 4:13 emphasis added).

When Jesus fed the multitude with the multiplication of loaves, John records, "When Jesus realized that they were about to come and take him by force to make him king, he withdrew again to the mountain by himself" (John 6:15, NRSV). It is the rare leader who by conviction will say, "If nominated, I will not run; if elected, I will not serve."

In Gethsemane's garden, moments before his arrest, Jesus prayed in anguish and trust:

Abba, Father, all things are possible to you.
Remove this cup from me!
Yet, not what I want, but what you want.
(Mark 14:36 [my translation])

He would not flee to safety; he would trust everything to God.

When Jesus was strapped and nailed to the cross, some jeered, "If you are the King of the Jews, save yourself" (Luke 23:37). Others said, "If you are the Son of God, come down from the cross" (Matthew 27:40). Others mocked, "He saved others; let him save himself, if he is the Christ of God" (Luke 23:35). Are these not echoes of the wilderness temptations?

But Jesus, who won the victory over the original temptations, would reaffirm those choices again and again. He would offer spiritual food. He would serve, not rule. He would trust his life and death into God's hands.

Yes, he would choose mission over security. He would not resort to the spectacular. He would die at the hands of violent power rather than take up violence. He would stay true to his mission as the Son of God and to the mission of the kingdom of God no matter what.

At the heart of these temptations were two: (1) to be more than the Spirit-filled son/servant of God and pretend to *be* God; and (2) to escape the demands of what it meant to be the son/servant of God. To put it another way: the temptation to be more than God has created and called us to be, or to be less. Jesus perceived who he was as the son/servant of God and the size of the stakes, and he chose to be who God created and called him to be.

Luke's Gospel then turns to the beginning of Jesus' ministry: "Then Jesus, filled with the power of the Spirit, returned to Galilee, and a report about him spread through all the surrounding country" (Luke 4:14, NRSV). With those words, we proceed to his ministry in Galilee.

NOTES

1. Diogenes Allen, *Temptation* (Princeton, NJ: Caroline Press, 1986), 14.

2. Fyodor Dostoevsky, *The Brothers Karamazov: A Novel in Four Parts with Epilogue*, trans. Richard Pevear and Larissa Volokhonsky (San Francisco: North Point Press, 1990), 254.

PART III

THE MINISTRY OF JESUS

6

JESUS AND THE REIGN OF GOD

The heart of Jesus' message and mission was what he called "the kingdom of God" or "reign of God." When I was growing up in evangelical Southern Baptist faith, the emphasis was on "eternal life," being "born again," and making sure you were going to end up in heaven. In contrast, Jesus' main message was about the kingdom of God coming to earth and our being part of it. (Matthew's reverent use of "kingdom of heaven" rather than "kingdom of God," which reflects Jewish reticence about the use of the name of God, has inadvertently reinforced a "heaven-oriented" faith.)

Mark begins the public ministry of Jesus fourteen verses into his Gospel with these words: "Jesus came to Galilee, proclaiming the good news of God and saying, 'The time is fulfilled, and the kingdom of God has come near; repent, and believe in the good news'" (Mark 1:14-15, NRSV). The kingdom of God, once seen as completely future and far away, has moved graciously and urgently near. It has the quality of unspeakably good news (*euangelion*). What was required to enter it or receive it was to "repent" and "believe."

REPENTANCE AND BELIEVING

The word *repent* may bring to us scalding shame, a counting of sins, some required change to be sure. But what change? And who decides? It is a guilt-inducing word. It sounds like a sudden police siren behind us as we drive.

But for Jesus, *repent* was a soaring, hopeful word, the sounding of trumpets across a canyon at dawn. The word *repent*, in the Hebrew tongue *shub*, means to turn or return to God. In the Hebrew mind, it meant not only an individual's turning, but also a nation's turning. And it meant not only a turn from idolatry or sin, but also a *re*turn to God their savior. It meant a return home from exile by the gracious and powerful help of God. In short, God was helping them turn and return.

The word for *repent* in New Testament Greek is *metanoia*, literally a change of mind, a turning of the mind. Jesus scholar Marcus Borg interprets it as "to go beyond the mind we have."[1] So repentance is not only about a turn from sin, but also about a turn from everything that can harm or bind us: fear, exile, injustice, blindness, despair, to name a few.

And what about "believing"? More than a believing this or that, it is a believing *in*. William Sloane Coffin writes, "*Credo*—I believe—best translates 'I have given my heart to.'"[2]

Believing is relational, involving, as Karen Armstrong suggests, trust, confidence, loyalty, engagement.[3] When Jesus talked about the kingdom, he spoke of entering it (Matthew 19:23), receiving it (Luke 18:17), and belonging to it (Mark 10:14); and of it being given (Luke 12:32), being seen (John 3:3), and coming upon (Luke 11:20).

The kingdom is a realm to which we are invited to belong: "Fear not, little flock, for it is your Father's good pleasure to give you the kingdom" (Luke 12:32). Faith, believing, is something more and something deeper than a set of beliefs, the recitation of a creed, or a doctrinal system. "Beliefs" are important to give structure or definition to our "believing," but these are secondary. Believing entails a relationship with the divine and a reorienting of one's life, a change in the way one lives one's life. It may come in an instant, or in degrees, as a flower turning its face to the sun.

THE KINGDOM OF GOD

Now to the main topic: the kingdom of God. Because it is the kingdom of *God*, and not our human kingdoms, it cannot be captured in human concepts and definitions. As partaking of the transcendent realm of God, it is both knowable and unknowable. The biblical idea of God is of a God who is self-revealing and mystery at the same time. Good theology is *kataphatic*; that is, it affirms who God is by using words, concepts, and images. And, good theology is *apophatic*; that is, it asserts what the divine is not, acknowledging that God dwells beyond words, concepts, images in silence and unknowing.

When Jesus spoke about the kingdom, his favorite way of teaching was in the metaphorical language of parables. He told uncountable ones. The kingdom is like a feast, a lost son, a woman baking bread, and on and on. The kingdom of God is like, is like, is like. The multiplicity of images, analogies, and stories preserved the mystery.

The multiplicity of metaphors continues. Martin Luther King Jr. called the kingdom the "beloved community." New Testament scholar Clarence Jordan called it "God's movement." Author and activist Wendell Berry calls it the "great economy" and goes on to say:

> The first principle of the kingdom of God is that it includes everything; in it the fall of every sparrow is a significant event. . . . Another principle, both ecological and traditional, is that everything in the kingdom of God is joined both to it and to everything else that is in it.[4]

Berry also calls it the "membership" where we live as true neighbors and kin, "members of one another," to use a phrase from Paul.

What did Jesus mean by the term? Jesus scholars John Dominic Crossan and Marcus Borg describe it as "God's passion for earth." I think Jesus meant by the term the space and time in the heavens and on earth where God reigns. The kingdom meant justice, joy, compassion, healing, and reconciliation. What has been broken is being made whole, what is wrong is set right. New Testament scholar Leander Keck calls it God's "rectifying impingement upon the world."[5]

In Hebrew Scripture the phrase *malkut shamayim* means "the royal reign" or "sole sovereignty" of God.[6] Surely Jesus had this meaning in mind when he spoke of the reign of God. Picture two partially overlapping circles. The circle on top is God's sole sovereignty and royal reign. The circle on the bottom is the created world, including our personal worlds. Where the circles overlap is when and where the kingdom has come.

For Jesus, the kingdom was where God reigns in healing, justice, joy, and peace. He invited all to join. Jesus' scandalous dinner parties with outcasts and sinners were a sign of the full welcome of this kingdom. So were his healings: "the blind receive their sight and the lame walk, lepers are cleansed and the deaf hear, and the dead are raised up, and the poor have good news preached to them" (Matthew 11:5).

Frederick Buechner describes the kingdom:

> The Kingdom of God is the time, or a time beyond time, when it will no longer be humans in their lunacy who are in charge of the world but God in his mercy who will be in charge of the world. It's the time above all else for wild rejoicing—like getting out of jail, like being cured of cancer, like finally at long last, coming home. And it is at hand, Jesus says.[7]

So, with joy, longing, and audacious hope Christians pray with Jesus, "Thy kingdom come . . . on earth as in heaven."

Now we come to what Jesus meant by "at hand." This issue divides scholars into opposing, sometimes vehemently so, camps. Was the kingdom of God fully here in the coming of Jesus, or was it, however near, still in the future? Was Jesus an apocalyptic prophet who believed that God would soon come, end history as we know it, and bring in a whole new world? Or did he believe that the kingdom had already dawned, not just *near* but *here*? Therefore all we need to do is to open our eyes and see it.[8]

Neither option is completely satisfactory. Scholars line up to debate the here-and-nowness of the kingdom versus the still-to-comeness of the kingdom. Jesus is quoted by each camp. Verses that speak to the here and now of the kingdom include these:

- "For the kingdom of God is among [*entos*] you" (Luke 17:21, NRSV)—"in your midst" (NIV), "within you" (KJV).
- "But if it is by the Spirit of God that I cast out demons, then the kingdom of God has come upon you" (Matthew 12:28).

Verses that speak to the kingdom to come include these:

- "Your kingdom come. Your will be done, on earth as it is in heaven" (Matthew 6:10, NRSV).
- "And then they will see the Son of man coming in clouds with great power and glory. . . . But of that day or that hour no one knows, not even the angels in heaven, nor the Son, but only the Father" (Mark 13:26,32).

The "already but not yet" quality of the kingdom of God is a paradox that cannot be resolved. It is a mystery that must be lived. Jesus saw the presence of the kingdom in the here and now, and he fervently looked for its final, complete coming.

So I offer a set of paradoxical motifs that express the nature of the kingdom of God. It is

> already but not yet;
> at hand but not in hand;[9]
> beyond this world but for this world;
> within us, between us, among us yet beyond us.

If the role of true religion is to help us experience reality in its fullest and most real, then we could say that the paradoxical nature of the when and where of God's kingdom corresponds to reality as we best know it—here in moments of justice and joy, healing wholeness and peace. And the kingdom is not yet here in the terrible absence of these things in injustice, illness, brokenness, anxiety, estrangement, and violence.

There is no doubt that Jesus believed that the kingdom of God was presently at work. It had drawn decisively near. And it seems clear that he looked for a full and final coming of the kingdom. So perhaps our spiritual posture as followers of Jesus is to be open to all the ways the kingdom of God is present now and to be faithful to the kingdom whose final coming in fullness is yet to be.

Biblical scholar Gerhard Lohfink says that the not-yetness of the kingdom is a result of our human "no" to its presence. There is a "hidden and humbled" shape of the kingdom because God has placed it in our hands to accept or reject.[10]

John Dominic Crossan stresses our human role in receiving the kingdom. He calls it "collaborative eschatology." The kingdom comes by divine-human collaboration. He quotes Desmond Tutu, who is paraphrasing Augustine: "God without us will not; as we without God cannot." Crossan follows, "Would it happen without God? No. Would it happen without believers? No."[11]

And yet it all begins with the gracious initiative of God and with Jesus as the agent of the God, in search of us and of the coming of the kingdom. Christine Tiez, a German theologian, commented at an international Bonhoeffer conference, "What is beyond this world is for this world."[12] Here "for" means two things: (1) the beyond is meant for earth, not just for heaven; and (2) God is for us, on the world's side as advocate, savior, friend, deliverer. This is the God Jesus revealed to us in his own life given radically for humanity, for us. Jesus came from God, for us. And the centrality of his message and mission was that the kingdom of God has drawn near.

NOTES

1. Marcus Borg, *Speaking Christian: Why Christian Words Have Lost Their Meaning and Power—And How They Can Be Restored* (New York: HarperOne, 2011), 15.

2. William Sloane Coffin, *Credo* (Louisville: Westminster John Knox Press, 2004), xv.

3. Karen Armstrong, *The Case for God* (New York: Knopf, 2009), 87ff.

4. Wendell Berry, "Two Economies," in Wendell Berry, *The Art of the Commonplace: Agrarian Essays of Wendell Berry*, ed. Norman Wirzba (Berkeley, CA: Counterpoint, 2002), 220, 235.

5. Leander Keck, *Who Is Jesus? History in the Perfect Tense* (Columbia: University of South Carolina Press, 2000), 81.

6. See Obery M. Hendricks Jr., *The Politics of Jesus: Rediscovering the True Revolutionary Nature of the Teachings of Jesus and How They Have Been Corrupted* (New York: Doubleday, 2006), 20–21; Gerhard Lohfink, *Jesus of Nazareth: What He Wanted, Who He Was*, trans. Linda M. Maloney (Collegeville, MN: Liturgical Press, 2012), 25.

7. Frederick Buechner, "The Kingdom of God," in Frederick Buechner, *The Clown in The Belfry: Writings on Faith and Fiction* (San Francisco: HarperSanFrancisco, 1992), 165.

8. For a full discussion of the options about "the coming of the kingdom," see E. P. Sanders, *The Historical Figure of Jesus* (New York: Penguin Books, 1993), 169–88.

9. The phrase of Christopher Morse, *The Difference Heaven Makes: Rehearing the Gospel as News* (London: T&T Clark, 2010), 6. He describes the "heaven" of the kingdom of heaven as "the course of God's forthcoming," p. 10.

10. Lohfink, *Jesus of Nazareth*, 22, 36–38.

11. John Dominic Crossan, *The Power of Parable: How Fiction by Jesus Became Fiction about Jesus* (New York: HarperOne, 2012), 135; also John Dominic Crossan, "Jesus and the Challenge of Collaborative Eschatology," in *The Historical Jesus: Five Views*, ed. James K. Beilby and Paul Rhodes Eddy (London: SPCK, 2010), 125.

12. At Union Theological Seminary, New York City, 2012.

7

THE COMMUNITY OF THE REIGN OF GOD

Very early in his ministry, Jesus began to call disciples to follow him. Nearly one hundred times in the Gospels we see the word *follow*. Discipleship was, above all else, about the following of Jesus. In the wilderness temptations he had clarified and confirmed his mission as the son/servant of God. He began to announce the thrilling news that the kingdom of God had drawn decisively, graciously near. But he needed a community as part of this mission, a community of the reign of God.

Jesus started with two, then two more, then twelve, but there were more than the Twelve.

CALLING THE TWELVE

Sixteen verses into Mark's Gospel, Jesus called the first two disciples. Passing by the Sea of Galilee, Jesus saw Simon (who would later be called Cephas, or Peter) and his brother, Andrew, casting their nets into the sea. "Follow me," Jesus said, "and I'll make you fishers for people." And the text says that "*immediately* they left their nets and followed him" (Mark 1:18 emphasis added).

Jesus had a genius for metaphor: fishing for people. There were at least two meanings: (1) rescuing people who were perishing in life's stormy seas; and (2) gathering people into the great net of the kingdom of God, first, "the lost sheep of the house of Israel," then beyond to the whole world. God needs a people. So do we.

Then Jesus called two more brothers, James and John, sons of Zebedee, who were in their boats mending their nets. He called them to follow, and, as Mark records, "they left their father Zebedee in the boat with the hired servants, and followed him" (Mark 1:20). One wonders what their father thought!

Here are two striking features of Jesus' call to his disciples. First, the call came at Jesus' initiative. They did not come to him as most students came to rabbis of that time, asking to be disciples. Jesus came to them. Second, the call required them to leave, at least temporarily, their families and homes to follow him on his mission.

Jesus' relationship with his disciples was more than the typical rabbi-student relationship. Jesus would teach them new ways to read Torah in light of the newly arriving kingdom of God. But he was calling them to more: to experience the presence of the reign of God and to join him in announcing and embodying this reign as they moved throughout Galilee.

Jesus' call was powerful and irresistible. It had an urgency and a fascination that drew them to leave their occupations, families, and homes to travel with him. Sometimes it was a following that involved a complete break with one's former life, such as for Levi the tax collector. Peter, on the other hand, kept contact with his home and his mother-in-law in Capernaum.

The word *disciple*, in Greek *mathētēs*, means "learner," but this kind of learning would involve everything in their lives. Although *mathētēs* means "learner," theologian Dallas Willard says that being a disciple may be best understood as being an "apprentice." An apprentice, he writes, "is simply someone who has decided to be with another person, under appropriate conditions, in order to become capable of doing what that person does or to become what that person is."[1] Indeed, Jesus would, at some point in his Galilean ministry, send his disciples out to do what he was doing: preach the kingdom, heal the sick, cast out demons.

Soon, the circle of four disciples (two sets of brothers) grew into a wider circle of disciples known as the Twelve. After Jesus called Levi to leave his life as a tax collector, Levi threw a party for his friends, including fellow tax collectors and other "sinners," and he invited Jesus to join them. The kingdom was gathering the whole people of God, not just from among the "righteous." The religious leaders complained to Jesus, "Why do you eat and drink with sinners?" He replied, "Those who are well have no need for a physician, but those who are sick; I have not come to call the righteous, but sinners to repentance" (Luke 5:31-32). Such radical inclusion would be an ongoing scandal.

So we have four fishermen and a tax collector, the latter of whom would be considered not only a "sinner," but also a cheat and a traitor. Soon Jesus filled out the circle of twelve:

1. Simon, whom Jesus nicknamed "Cephas" (in Aramaic) or "Peter" (in Greek), which means "rock";
2. Andrew, Simon's brother;
3. James, the son of Zebedee, and
4. John, the son of Zebedee, the brothers whom Jesus nicknamed "sons of thunder" (Mark 3:17), perhaps for their tempestuous personalities;
5. Philip, who appears in John's Gospel but is mentioned in the list of disciples in Matthew, Mark, and Luke;
6. Bartholomew, known only by the lists in Matthew, Mark, and Luke, identified by some scholars as the Nathanael of John's Gospel (see John 1:45-49);

7. Thomas, called "the Twin," but most often remembered as the doubter for his insistence on seeing and touching the Risen Christ before he believed (John 20:25);

8. Matthew (Levi in the call stories in Mark 2:14 and Luke 5:27), the tax collector;

9. James, the son of Alphaeus, known only by the list;

10. Thaddaeus, known only by the lists in Matthew and Mark; the lists in Luke and Acts (written by the same author) substitute Judas, the son of James, for Thaddeus;

11. Simon, the Cananean or Zealot (in Aramaic, the word *qu'ana* means "zealous" or "jealous" for God, so it was transliterated as "Cananean" and translated as "Zealot");[2]

12. Judas Iscariot, who would betray Jesus and "hand him over" to the authorities.

What was the significance of Jesus calling *twelve*? It was a symbolic prophetic act. The Twelve represented the regathering of the twelve tribes of Israel as part of the inbreaking kingdom of God. The prophets Isaiah (Isaiah 11:12), Jeremiah (Jeremiah 31:1), and Ezekiel (Ezekiel 34) had dreamed God's dream of the final coming of the kingdom, which would begin with the ingathering of the twelve tribes of Israel.[3] From the regathered Israel would come the gathering of all people to God, a universal vision: "For my house shall be called a house of prayer for all peoples. . . . I will gather others besides those already gathered" (Isaiah 56:7-8, NRSV). Foreigners and eunuchs will also be included along with all those formerly excluded by race, nationality, or cultic impurity.

THE BROADER CIRCLE OF DISCIPLES

The intimate circle of Jesus' disciples included more, however, than the Twelve. Shockingly, it also included women. Luke's Gospel remembers this startling fact:

Soon afterwards he went on through cities and villages, proclaiming and bringing the good news of the kingdom of God. The twelve were with him, as well as some women who had been cured of evil spirits and infirmities: Mary, called Magdalene, from whom seven demons had gone out, and Joanna, the wife of Herod's steward Chuza, and Susanna, and many others, who provided for them out of their resources. (Luke 8:1-3, NRSV)

So we add Mary Magdalene, who has been miscast in church tradition as a prostitute and who may have had a unique closeness to Jesus and a leadership role in the early Christian community. And we also include Susanna and Joanna, whose husband was Herod's steward (Luke 8:3). What a story that must have been! Herod had beheaded John the Baptist, and later in Jesus' ministry some Pharisees (yes, Pharisees) came to Jesus and warned him that Herod was a danger to him as well (Luke 13:31). Now the wife of Herod's steward is a follower of Jesus. Did Chuza approve of her choice? Did he have to keep it secret?

Then there were others close to Jesus whom we could call "residential members" of the Jesus movement.[4] They opened their homes to Jesus and his disciples. Prominent among this group was the Bethany family of Mary and Martha and their brother, Lazarus. Their home may have been Jesus' stopover on his trips to Jerusalem. The Gospels of Luke and John note the closeness of their friendship to Jesus, how he loved them and they him (Luke 10:38-40; John 11:1-44). Similarly, Peter's house in Capernaum may well have been Jesus' "headquarters" in Galilee (Matthew 8:14-15).

There were the "occasional helpers" of Jesus,[5] including Joseph of Arimathea, a member of the Jewish Sanhedrin who later asked permission for the body of Jesus and buried him in his own tomb (see Luke 23:50-53).

There were also "seekers" fascinated by Jesus who came to learn from him, such as Nicodemus (John 3:1-15). There were even a few who were healed or delivered from demons, grateful people who tried to tag along with Jesus after their miracle. (Jesus told most of these to go back to their homes.)

Finally, there were the crowds (*ochloi*) that followed Jesus, the size of which became a threat in the minds of political and religious leaders who worried over the uneasy "peace" between Israel and Rome. In the *ochloi* were people of widely different levels of commitment to the way of Jesus. Jesus called *all* to join him in the reign of God, which was graciously and urgently at hand. He opened himself to inquirers and seekers. He did not look down his nose at them. But, he did not call everyone to be the kind of disciple who followed him on the road.

One specific episode comes to mind. There was a man, unnamed, who was going around healing people in the name of Jesus. The disciples came to Jesus and asked him to stop the man. Jesus replied, "Do not stop him; for no one who does a deed of power in my name will be able soon afterward to speak evil of me. *Whoever is not against us is for us*" (Mark 9:39-40, NRSV [emphasis added]).

There were then and are today many different kinds of people following Jesus and many different forms of following. Might we take encouragement, not offense, in this? Jesus guides us in the answer. He did not accept just one kind of follower. Each one of us is called to find our own unique path of discipleship.

A Hasidic tale records the thought of Rabbi Zusya. The aging rabbi said, "In the coming world, they will not ask me: 'Why were you not Moses?' They will ask me: 'Why were you not Zusya?'"[6] Jesus too calls us by name.

Wherever we are on the journey with Jesus, whether an inquirer, one who has left all to follow, or one who is growing in what it means to be a follower, Jesus welcomes us all. Who knows where our fascination with Jesus will lead?

What is clear is that God needs not just individuals; God needs a community, a people. And we need a community.

The reign of God requires a concrete social location and a communal experience, a particular and real community. We have our solitary moments along the path in our following of Jesus, but it is not a solitary journey.

Often in contemporary America, we think of spirituality in individualistic terms: "I'm spiritual but not religious." We may take pride in the uniqueness of our particular spiritual path. We are, however, created for communion and community—with one another and with God. We cannot get where we need to go by ourselves. As John Wesley put it, "No one gets to heaven alone."

NOTES

1. Dallas Willard, *The Divine Conspiracy: Rediscovering Our Hidden Life in God* (San Francisco: HarperSanFrancisco, 1998), 282.

2. The word *zealot* would have referred to a group zealous to protect the purity of God's laws or the growing group whose zeal for God's sole sovereignty led them to political and violent resistance to Rome under the banner "Only God is king." Whether a religious or a political zealot, Simon would have undergone transformational change when he joined Jesus' circle of disciples. He would have seen Jesus welcome sinners, tax collectors, and prostitutes into the kingdom, something unthinkable for someone zealous to protect God's law; and, Jesus' preaching of nonviolence and love for the enemy would have stood apart from the nascent Zealot movement, which favored violent resistance against the Roman oppressor.

3. See John P. Meier, *A Marginal Jew: Rethinking the Historical Jesus*, vol. 3, *Companions and Competitors* (New York: Doubleday, 2001), 148–54; Gerhard Lohfink, *Jesus of Nazareth: What He Wanted, Who He Was*, trans. Linda M. Maloney (Collegeville, MN: Liturgical Press, 2012), 38–71.

4. Lohfink, *Jesus of Nazareth*, 91–93.

5. Ibid., 93.

6. Parker Palmer, *Let Your Life Speak: Listening for the Voice of Vocation* (San Francisco: Jossey-Bass, 2000), 11.

8

JESUS THE HEALER

The kingdom of God means many things: justice, joy, compassion, radical inclusion, peace, reconciliation, home. It means *healing* too. Jesus was a healer and exorcist, a worker of "startling deeds," according to the Jewish historian Josephus. Mark's Gospel begins the ministry of Jesus with a raft of healings: one exorcism and two healings plus a report of numerous others—all before Mark ends his first chapter.

Similarly, Matthew describes the beginning of Jesus' ministry: "Jesus went throughout Galilee, teaching in their synagogues and proclaiming the good news of the kingdom and curing every disease and every sickness among the people" (Matthew 4:23, NRSV).

New Testament scholar Obery Hendricks comments, "Throughout his ministry, Jesus treated the people and their needs as holy by healing their bodies, their souls, their psyche."[1] We must not minimize Jesus' role as a healer.

HEALING IN THE GOSPELS

Jesus not only healed every kind of illness; he healed *anybody* who came to be healed—Jew, Gentile, sinner, righteous, man, woman, and child. He never made a moral demand on persons before healing them. The only requirement was that they recognize their need and have enough faith to crack the door open to God's grace. Sometimes, God cracked the door open for them.

Jesus' healings were more than physical: he healed minds, emotions, spirits too. Why did he heal? Over and over again, the answer was simply his compassion. Out of God's tender mercies he healed them—and in the power of God's spirit manifest as the kingdom drew near.

In Matthew's Gospel alone, we see seventeen individuals healed:

> a leper
> a centurion's paralyzed servant
> Peter's feverish mother-in-law
> two men possessed by demons
> a paralyzed man
> the daughter of Jairus, given up for dead
> a woman with a flow of blood
> two blind men
> a mute demoniac
> a man with a withered hand
> a blind and mute demoniac
> a Canaanite woman's daughter possessed by a demon
> a man's epileptic son
> two more blind men[2]

Then there were thirteen descriptions of groups being healed:

> the lame
> the deaf
> a hungry multitude (yes, feeding is a miracle too, a social
>   miracle)
> people with seizures
> the maimed
> the mute

lepers
the paralyzed
those with evil spirits
those harassed and helpless
those trapped in sin
those walking in the shadow of death[3]

How many ways are there to be a leper, paralyzed, blind, mute, deaf, maimed, heart-sick, soul-sick, sin-sick? Jesus healed all maladies. Out of his compassion, as wide as the skies, he healed them.

Healing is not an incidental part of the Gospels. If you took scissors and cut all the New Testament miracles out of your Bible, it would look like the sheet of paper after paper dolls have been cut out. President Thomas Jefferson did just that in 1804! But John P. Meier, a first-rank historical Jesus scholar, concludes after extensive research into the matter:

> I use the criteria of historicity to establish the global assertion that, during his public ministry, Jesus claimed to work miracles, that Jesus was thought to work miracles by his contemporaries, friend and foes alike, and that Jesus did indeed do some extraordinary deeds that his adversaries explained by claiming that he was in league with demonic powers. . . . A completely non-miraculous Jesus, an idea propagated by Enlightenment thinkers like Thomas Jefferson, is a prime example of recasting a first-century prophet to fit the sensibilities of a modern intellectual elite.[4]

Jesus as a healer prompts many questions. Was Jesus' healing power unique in the ancient world? No. Can he, in the power of the Spirit, heal today? Many would answer yes. Did Jesus' healings involve the breaking of "natural laws"? This is a peculiarly modern question.

One way that scholars since the Enlightenment have approached the historicity of Jesus' miracles is to conclude that only what is possible today in our understanding of healing was possible then. In other words, "What does not happen now did not happen then." Such a position whittles the story of Jesus down to what we can understand. Others say that Jesus did his work in an age of miracles, but that age is over. Neither of these solutions seems satisfactory.

In the Bible there are surprising miracles and everyday miracles. Gerhard Lohfink describes the former:

> For the Bible a miracle is something unusual, inexplicable, incomprehensible, disturbing, unexpected, shocking, something that amazes and that explodes the ordinary, something by which God plucks people out of their indifference and causes them to look at him.[5]

Jesus offered such surprising, dramatic miracles to people in their great need.

But there are also everyday miracles, miracles in the ordinary. The Bible calls these "blessings"—the gift of children, the regular mendings of the body that we take for granted, daily provision and sustenance. These everyday miracles too are from the hand of God. Jesus urged his followers to open their eyes to the everyday miracles and live with gratitude.

We do not need to believe that God suspends natural law *as we understand it* in order to heal. Gerhard Lohfink says that a miracle is "only a special case of God's constant work in the world."[6]

> If we see a miracle as part of what God has always been graciously bringing about in the world, we must say that a genuine miracle is done by God, but precisely not in such a way that God sets aside human action and the laws of nature. Rather, every miracle is at the same time always bringing to the fore what human and nature are able to do. Natural laws are not broken but elevated to a higher level. The miracle exalts nature; it does not bore holes in it.

It does not destroy the natural order of things but brings it to fulfillment.[7]

The miracles of Jesus were a "special case of God's constant work." Most of the time, they required the "faith" of the person being healed, faith if only the size of a mustard seed. Faith is an act of trust as concrete as traveling to see Jesus, as recognizing one's needs and crying out, "Lord, help me."

What about when we are not healed even though we have great faith? Theologian Frank Tupper's wife, Betty, died of breast cancer despite great faith and many prayers. In an unpublished essay, Tupper concluded, "Faith cannot open a door that is not there, but it can help us walk through an open door that most people cannot see."

Miracles are moments of unusual partnership between God and people. A healing may be dramatic or commonplace, seen or unseen. This may occur in body, mind, or spirit. In some cases, we can be "healed" at a deep level of mind and spirit but not cured physically.

A HEALING STORY

I present one healing story, Mark 5:21-43. It is an intricately woven narrative, a miracle within a miracle, two healings—one of a twelve-year-old girl, the other of a woman sick for twelve years. They show Jesus the healer at work.

Jairus, the leader of the local synagogue, came to Jesus, knelt down, and pleaded with Jesus to come to his house and heal his daughter, who was near death. Life does not get more real and desperate than that. He was experiencing what the poet T. S. Eliot described as "the purification of the motive / In the ground of our beseeching.[8] The father was at the *ground of the ground* of his beseeching. *Please, Jesus, help.*

At the end of the story, we learn that the girl was twelve. Why does this detail pull at my heart? Is it because I've been the father of a twelve-year-old girl and the brother of one?

Do you remember when you were twelve? The summer when you turned twelve?

Is it the thought that the very God who created this vast universe would notice a twelve-year-old child? That God cares not just for the world, and for Israel, but also for a pre-teen middle-school-aged girl who has gotten very sick?

Jesus does not hesitate; he starts out immediately for the girl's house.

While Jesus is en route, a second figure enters the scene: a woman chronically ill with "a flow of blood for twelve years." We do not know the exact diagnosis, but her story is a long trail of tears and disappointment. Her flow of blood rendered her ritually unclean, unable to go to the temple, unable to touch or be touched without making others unclean. Perhaps she was childless. She may have been divorced by her husband or estranged from her family because of her condition. She has been from physician to physician with no cure, and now her funds are exhausted. It is the plight of many sick in our nation today.

Those who suffer chronic illness often are passed from doctor to doctor. They often are beset by self-judgment on top of the judgments of those around them. Why can't she get well? Why can't *I* get well? Has my faith not been strong enough? Have I not practiced my visualization technique rigorously enough?

This woman had heard of the wonders that Jesus had been performing. Could he help her? She moved toward him from behind so he wouldn't see her, so the crowd wouldn't notice her. She touched the fringes of his garment, the 613 tassels worn by observant Jewish men. *If I touch his garments I will be made well*, she thought, with a hope that may have even taken her by surprise. Like the character in Samuel Beckett's absurdist play, *Waiting for Godot*: "I can't go on, I'll go on."

Immediately, when she touched those fringes, she "knew in her body" that she had been healed. Just as suddenly, Jesus felt a "streaming power" go out of him, through him to her.

The phrase "knew in her body" is an evocative one. It is important in the healing process to pay attention to the body, to seek its wisdom, to learn what it is trying to say to you. And note the streaming power that Jesus felt leave him. It was the divine power streaming from God through him to the woman. Jesus was a vessel, in this case an unconscious vessel. He did not know that she had touched his garment, had come for healing.

Jesus, the healer, is healer only and inasmuch as he is the power and presence of God to that person, and he is the instrument of the larger healing ministry of God available to all persons throughout the world through the Spirit of God.

"Daughter," he said to her, "your faith has made you well." He was restoring her to daughterhood, beloved daughter of God and daughter of Abraham. And she had made herself available to the power and presence of God by believing in Jesus as the power and presence of God to her.

Then Jesus headed on toward the home of Jairus. On the way, a messenger came with the news that the girl had died. Jesus proceeded toward his destination anyway.

When he arrived, a crowd was already gathered in full funeral mode, weeping and wailing. Jesus responded, "Why the commotion, the weeping and wailing? The child is not dead but sleeping." Then we get this startling detail: "The crowd laughed at him." It was the laughter of cynicism. This was not healing laughter but the brittle laughter of self-defense. They'd already determined what was possible and not possible. Sometimes our disappointment leads us there—too much heartbreak, too many unanswered prayers.

Then the text says something even more startling: Jesus *put them out.* Jesus the bouncer! He told them to get out of the house.

So now, there were in the house just Jesus, the parents, the girl, and three disciples, Peter, James, and John. Jesus took her hand. "*Talitha koum,*" he said, Aramaic for "Little girl, rise." And she rose and walked around. And Jesus said, "Get her something to eat."

Sometimes people think we're dead when we're not. Sometimes we think we're dead when we're not, and Jesus the healer, the resurrection and the life, comes and says, "Rise!"

Czeslaw Milosz, a Nobel Prize–winner in literature, heard this story read one Sunday in church and responded:

> *This is for me. To make me rise from the dead*
> *And repeat the hope of those who lived before me.*[9]

This miracle and all the miracles in the Gospels are for us, to help us rise from the dead, believe more deeply, and hope with those who have believed before us.

NOTES

1. Obery M. Hendricks Jr., *The Politics of Jesus: Rediscovering the True Revolutionary Nature of the Teachings of Jesus and How They Have Been Corrupted* (New York: Doubleday, 2006), 108.

2. Individual healings: Matthew 8:1-4; 8:5-13; 8:14-15; 8:28-32; 9:2-8; 9:18-19,23-26; 9:20-22; 9:27-31; 9:32-34; 12:9-13; 12:22; 15:21-28; 17:14-18; 20:29-34.

3. Group healings: Matthew 4:23-24; 8:16-17; 9:35-36; 10:8; 11:5; 12:15; 14:14; 14:34-36; 15:30; 15:32-39.

4. John P. Meier, *A Marginal Jew: Rethinking the Historical Jesus*, vol. 2, *Mentor, Message, and Miracles* (New York: Doubleday, 1994), 12.

5. Gerhard Lohfink, *Jesus of Nazareth: What He Wanted, How He Was*, trans. Linda M. Maloney (Collegeville, MN: Liturgical Press, 2012), 140.

6. Ibid., 141.

7. Ibid.

8. T. S. Eliot, "Little Gidding," in T. S. Eliot, *Four Quartets* (New York: Houghton Mifflin Harcourt, 1971), 57.

9. Czeslaw Milosz, "With Her," in Czeslaw Milosz, *Selected Poems, 1931–2004* (New York: HarperCollins, 2006), 197.

9

JESUS THE EXORCIST

Perhaps the most foreign dimension of Jesus' ministry was his power to free people from what were variously called evil spirits, demons, or unclean spirits—Jesus the exorcist. It is a long journey back in time to where demons were considered part of daily life. "The past is a foreign country: they do things differently there," to quote L. P. Hartley again.[1]

In Jesus' day, if you were sick or deeply disturbed in spirit, the cause often was seen as the work of Satan and his legion of demons. The boundary of the self was permeable, vulnerable to spirits good and evil.

Think "germs." Today we think the cause of much illness is germs. We cannot see them with the naked eye, but we believe in them. So with demons in Jesus' day. Disturbances in body, mind, and spirit were seen as due to unclean spirits invisibly but powerfully inhabiting the world.

Therefore in Jesus' day, maladies of body, mind, and spirit were cured through exorcism, the power of God driving the lesser powers of evil out. In some parts of the world and in some expressions of Christianity, exorcism and "deliverance" ministries continue to be major practices today.

What seems foreign about exorcism may have a profound point of contact in what we call "self-psychology," the study of disturbances in the self and pathways to healing.

We can speak of the "divided self" or "split self." There are the "idealized self" that we promote to other people and the "disinherited self" that we push into the shadows (or project onto others). The hope for healing is, in theologian Parker Palmer's words, to be "divided no more."

We may also speak of the "true self" and the "false self." The true self is the self created and sustained by God. The false self is the self that we create, shaped by the world around us. The false self is full of compulsions. What the church began to refer to as the seven deadly sins—pride, sloth, envy, anger, greed, gluttony, and lust—can be seen as compulsions of the false self. In Jesus' day, these were seen as the work of demonic powers.

Feminist philosopher Luce Irigaray writes about "the dissolved self," whereby people dissolve their selfhood in serving other's needs and lose the container of the self. The result is the lack of a sure sense of self.[2]

We can speak of the "defended self," which spends enormous energy defending the self, promoting its righteousness and superiority. The world thus becomes divided into good (me, us) and evil (you, them).

The New Testament speaks of "the principalities and powers," suprapersonal forces that shape and dominate our lives: racism, rankism, nationalism, sexism, anti-Semitism, and other ideologies that distort our picture of the world and cause harm.

One can experience a moral disturbance when acting contrary to one's own values. A repressed or shadow side then rises powerfully to the surface and causes us to act in unhealthy and destructive ways.

What is the hope for the self? "Is there no balm in Gilead? Is there no physician there?" (Jeremiah 8:22)? In his poem "Hagia Sophia," Thomas Merton writes, "There is in all visible things an invisible fecundity . . . a hidden wholeness."[3]

The hope is in that true self created in the image of God, beloved of God, but sometimes deeply hidden. There is "a hidden wholeness," and Jesus takes us there.

In an interview with Krista Tippett, host of the radio show and podcast *On Being*, Irish poet and philosopher John O'Donohue said,

> Your identity is not equivalent to your biography. . . . There is a place in you where you have never been wounded, where there is still a sureness in you, where there is a seamlessness in you, and where there is a confidence and tranquility in you. . . . The intention of prayer and spirituality and love is now and again to visit that inner kind of sanctuary.[4]

Jesus the exorcist, the healer, leads us there.

EXORCISMS AND DEMONS

In Mark's Gospel, the first exorcism happens twenty-three verses from the beginning (Mark 1:23-26). A man with an unclean spirit was in the synagogue. The evil spirit cried out to Jesus, whom it recognized as someone with the power to cast him out: "What have you to do to us, Jesus of Nazareth? . . . I know who you are, the Holy One of God." Jesus rebuked the spirit and said, "Be silent, and come out of him!" And the loud, noisy, clamorous spirit came out.

One of the most dramatic and poignant of Jesus' exorcisms was of the Gerasene demoniac (Mark 5:1-20). The man's condition was a horror. He lived wild among the tombs, the dead. The townspeople tried to restrain him with chains, which he broke again and again. He wandered among the graves, naked, howling, slashing himself with stones.

I've seen that spirit of self-mutilation in people. I know it in myself. Sometimes the only kind of hate we will let ourselves feel is self-hate.

I remember a traumatized daughter of God who came into my office. She rolled up her sleeves and showed me hundreds of tiny scars where she had cut herself over the years. Did the pain of the razor blade distract her from a more terrible psychic pain? What was the underlying pain? We cut ourselves in all kinds of ways.

When Jesus approached the man—and the approach itself was an act of grace—the man cried out in terror, "Son of the Most High God . . . do not torment me." All he could imagine from God was God coming to judge, God coming as torment. Sometimes our images of God lead us to flee God when we most need God. The man was drawing back from Jesus' approach, saying, in effect, "Do not look at me. Do not touch me."

Jesus ordered the unclean spirit out: "Come out of the man!" Jesus asked the spirit's name. "My name is Legion, for we are many." In the Roman military, a legion usually had six thousand soldiers. As Eugene Peterson translates it, "My name is Mob!" (Mark 5:9, MSG). Have you ever felt like Mob was inside you?

When C. S. Lewis was moving toward his conversion to Christianity, the Spirit of God revealed to him the state of his soul. It was not a pleasant revelation. "What I saw there," Lewis wrote, "appalled me." He went on to describe the vision: "a zoo of lusts, a bedlam of ambitions, a nursery of fears, a harem of fondled hatreds. My name was Legion."[5]

After Jesus commanded the unclean spirits to come out, we are given a beautiful picture of this man healed. He was sitting at Jesus' feet, "clothed and in his right mind" (Mark 5:15, NRSV). He had been reconnected to his hidden wholeness. Miraculous!

The neighbors, however, were not pleased. The demons had run into a herd of (unclean) pigs that ran into the sea and drowned. The townspeople were angry with Jesus and asked him to leave. They were not ready to receive this healed man back into their society. A community can become all too comfortable identifying who is "sick" and banishing those individuals to places like the tombs. We are more comfortable with having the mentally ill, the criminal "sinners," the scary ones, put away somewhere. We do not want them back.

A healing can upset the equilibrium of a community segregated into zones for the good and bad, the sick and the well, the poor and the wealthy. Jesus upsets the equilibrium of every society based on such divisions. As South African theologians declared to the world, "Apartheid is heresy."

Healing needs to happen at all levels of being: the inner world of the self, as well as in the family, the community, the church, synagogue, temple, and mosque, the nation and the world of nations.

DELIVERED FOR DISCIPLESHIP

I offer one more healing story from the Gospels: the deliverance of Mary Magdalene from seven demons (Luke 8:2). It is told in a single verse, and Luke gives us no details. We assume that Jesus cast them out. Her larger story as one of the faithful disciples is all the more fascinating because she enjoyed a singularly intimate relationship with Jesus and was the first to whom he appeared as the Risen Christ (John 20:11-18). The noncanonical *Gospel of Mary* suggests that she had a leadership role in an early Christian community.

What were her demons? The Gospels are silent. Since the sixth century, lascivious male minds have projected sexual sins onto her, and she has been miscast as a repentant prostitute. In 594 CE, Pope Gregory the Great conflated three biblical women's stories in the Gospels into one and so identified Mary Magdalene as the prostitute who came to anoint Jesus' feet. Here is the projection of an androcentric culture, hysterical about sexuality and all too eager to demonize women. Cultural and psychological healing is needed here.

The seven demons could have been any major disruption in her personhood. The number seven may have symbolized the severity of her disruption.

Did she suffer a divided self, a split self, an addicted self, a dissolved self? We cannot know, but she was delivered of her demons, and she became a fervent follower of Jesus.

What was true for the Gerasene demoniac was true for Mary Magdalene. She had become *one*. Atonement, at-one-ment, had happened—with God and within herself. She had discovered the "hidden wholeness," the place where she had never been wounded.

The great Hebrew confession of faith, the *Shema*, declares:

Shema Yisrael
Hear, O Israel
Adonai Eloheinu
The Lord is our God
Adonai Echad
The Lord is one.

If we affirm this as true, that God is *one,* then perhaps we too can be *one*. Jesus prayed in John's Gospel that we might be one with God as he was (John 17:11), one with God, one inside one's self, one with others. Ancient Syriac Christianity called Jesus *Ihidaya*, which means Single One, Unified One, Whole One.[6] When oneness happens, healing happens. This is who Jesus was and what he brought.

NOTES

1. L. P. Hartley, *The Go-Between* (1953; repr., New York: New York Review of Books, 2002), 17.

2. Serene Jones, *Feminist Theory and Christian Theology: Cartographies of Grace* (Minneapolis: Fortress Press, 2000), 120–21.

3. Thomas Merton, "Hagia Sophia," in Thomas Merton, *Thomas Merton, Spiritual Master: The Essential Writings*, ed. Lawrence S. Cunningham (New York: Paulist Press, 1992), 258.

4. "John O'Donohue: The Inner Landscape of Beauty," *On Being*, August 6, 2015, http://www.onbeing.org/program/john-odonohue-the-inner-landscape-of-beauty /transcript/7801#main_content.

5. C. S. Lewis, *Surprised by Joy* (New York: Harcourt, Brace, 1955), 226.

6. Cynthia Bourgeault, *The Wisdom Jesus: Transforming Heart and Mind; A New Perspective on Christ and His Message* (Boston: Shambhala, 2008), 21.

10

JESUS AND COMPASSION

The Dalai Lama, worldwide leader of Tibetan Buddhism, when asked about his religion, replied, "My religion is very simple. My religion is kindness."

We could—or should—say the same thing about the religion of Jesus: it is a religion of kindness. The predominant biblical word for it is *compassion*. The religion of Jesus is a religion of compassion. Jesus himself was the divine compassion made flesh.

If you look up the word compassion in Webster's dictionary, you get this definition: "the deep feeling for and understanding of misery or suffering and the concomitant desire to promote its alleviation." It's not enough to feel for another's suffering or misery; we must seek to understand it. And it's not enough to understand it; one must seek to alleviate it, or at least bring comfort.

That's a good start, but if you want to see compassion in action, watch Jesus in the Gospels. In fact, in the Gospels, the Greek word for "compassion" is used only in reference to God and Jesus. (Well, almost, as we will see.)

The Greek word for "compassion" is *splanchnon*, or in its verbal form, *splanchnizomai*, "to have compassion." It is literally the word for one's inner organs or bowels, and it means to be moved at the deepest places of the self. We might substitute "heart" today. In the Hebrew and Aramaic, which Jesus spoke, the word is the plural of the word for "womb."[1] The divine compassion is womb-like, as a mother's love for a child. We have biblical phrases such as the "tender mercies" and "loving-kindness" of God.

Over and over, Jesus is described in the Gospels as compassion in action:

> And Jesus went about all the cities and villages, teaching in their synagogues and preaching the gospel of the kingdom, and healing every disease and every infirmity. When he saw the crowds, he *had compassion* for them, because they were harassed and helpless, like sheep without a shepherd. (Matthew 9:35-36 emphasis added)

To those sick in body, mind, and spirit, Jesus' compassion issued into healing: "As he went ashore he saw the great throng; and he *had compassion* on them, and healed their sick" (Matthew 14:14 emphasis added). A leper came to Jesus and pleaded, "If you want to, you can make me clean." And Jesus was "moved with compassion." Jesus answered, "I do want to," and he touched this untouchable man and healed him (Mark 1:40-42).

Once, Jesus saw the body of a young man being carried out of a house, the only son of a widow. He "had compassion" on her and brought the son back to life (Luke 7:11-17).

There's more. Jesus had compassion for a large crowd that had gathered to hear him preach and now were hungry. He said to his disciples, "*I have compassion* on the crowd . . . and I am unwilling to send them away hungry lest they faint on the way" (Matthew 15:32 emphasis added). So he fed them, multiplying the loaves and fish. God's compassion wants the hungry fed.

Jesus' compassion also reached out to those buffeted by life, to those who had lost their way, "harassed and helpless, like sheep without a shepherd" (Matthew 9:36). He offered these words of invitation: "Come to me, all who labor and are heavy laden, and I will give you rest" (Matthew 11:28).

To the lost he showed the way home, to those languishing in despair he brought hope. To the purposeless he brought meaning.

But that's not all. Above, I wrote that the word for "compassion" in the Gospels was used only in reference to Jesus and God. That's not quite right. Jesus used the word to describe the actions of characters in his two most famous parables.

In the first parable (Luke 10:29-37), a man going down from Jerusalem to Jericho fell among thieves who robbed him and beat him and left him half dead. Two Jewish religious officials came by, and each of them ignored the man and his need. Then a hated Samaritan came by and saw him and "had compassion" on him. He bandaged the man's wounds, put him on his donkey, and walked him to an inn, where he nursed the man through the night. The next day he paid for the night's stay and pledged to pay whatever the man's future expenses might be.

In the second parable (Luke 15:11-32), the younger of two sons asked his father for his inheritance and left home. It was a horrendously disrespectful thing to do. The young man went to a "far country," where he squandered his inheritance in "loose living." Then one day, in desperate straits, he "came to himself" and returned home to beg his father to take him back, not as a son, but as a hired hand. The father saw him at a distance and "had compassion" on him and ran to him and embraced and kissed him, welcoming him home as a son and calling for a homecoming feast. God's compassion is like that.

The way of Jesus was the way of compassion, the kindness of God. And this way became the way of those who followed Jesus. They, touched by the kindness of the Lord, lived that kindness in relationship with one another.

A major command in the Hebrew Scriptures is "Be holy, because I am holy" (Leviticus 11:44, NRSV). Jesus instead commanded his disciples, "Be merciful [compassionate] just as your Father is merciful [compassionate]" (Luke 6:36, NRSV). (In Matthew 5:48, Jesus' command is to be "perfect as your heavenly Father is perfect." Here, "perfect" means complete or whole.)

Marcus Borg has deepened our understanding of the profound shift that Jesus was offering from a "politics of holiness" to a "politics of compassion."[2] The Pharisees of the day offered "salvation through purity." In order to stay pure, people had to divide the world into pure and impure, clean and unclean zones. A "purity map," as Borg calls it, was drawn to separate one from another.

Circumstances of one's birth could determine which zone a person was in. Was an individual's birth legitimate or illegitimate? Whole or impaired? Male or female? Jew or Gentile?

The map had to do with ritual cleanness. Who was observing all 613 laws of the Torah? Who made the proper sacrifice? Who could *afford* to make a sacrifice? A person's profession could be deemed unclean: tax collector, prostitute, swineherd. Samaritans were doubly unclean: their ancestors had intermarried with non-Jews and had relaxed the law of Moses. The purity map governed all parts of one's life, which is why Borg calls it "the politics of holiness."

In contradistinction, Jesus brought a "politics of compassion" that brought "salvation through wholeness." It began in the compassion of God.

One day Jesus was eating at a Pharisee's house—which showed his compassion toward Pharisees too. A woman on the wrong side of the purity maps—a female, a sinner, possibly a prostitute ("a woman of the city" in Luke 7:37)—came into the room. What gave her the courage to come to him? Had she already seen the compassion of Jesus in action?

On that day, she entered the room carrying an alabaster box of perfumed oil to anoint his feet. Her tears just fell. They spilled down her face and wet Jesus' feet. She let down her hair and dried his feet with her hair; then she kissed his feet and anointed them with her perfume.

The Pharisee was scandalized that she would do such a thing, and that Jesus would *let* her do it. Jesus knew what he was thinking, and so he told this story: A creditor had two debtors, one owed him about $5,000; the other, $500 (see Luke 7:41, TLB). When neither creditor could pay, he freely forgave them both. "Which would love him more?" Jesus asked the Pharisee. The Pharisee answered, "I suppose the one who was forgiven the greater debt." "You have answered correctly," Jesus said, and then he drove the point home:

> Do you see this woman? I entered your house, you gave me no water for my feet, but she has wet my feet with her tears and wiped them with her hair. You gave me no kiss, but from the time I came in, she has not ceased to kiss my feet. You did not anoint my head with oil, but she has anointed my feet with ointment. Therefore I tell you, her sins, which are many, are forgiven, for she loved much; but he who is forgiven little, loves little. (Luke 7:44-47)

Then Jesus turned from the Pharisee (whose roasted lamb had probably just gotten stuck in his throat) to the woman and said the words that she'd already heard, words that had brought her there and brought her tears, words that had let down her hair and brought her lips to his feet, words that were life to her: "Your sins are forgiven." Then this: "Your faith has made you whole. Go in peace."

Compassion was the way of Jesus. He poured it out on the sick, the sinner, the outcast, the wandering, harassed, and helpless like sheep without a shepherd. A nineteenth-century hymn by Frederick W. Faber captures the nature of God:

There's a wideness in God's mercy,
Like the wideness of the sea;

> *There's a kindness in His justice,*
> *Which is more than liberty.*
>
> *For the love of God is broader*
> *Than the measure of our mind;*
> *And the heart of the Eternal*
> *Is most wonderfully kind.*

So Jesus showed us.

NOTES

1. Marcus J. Borg, *Meeting Jesus Again for the First Time: The Historical Jesus and the Heart of Contemporary Faith* (San Francisco: HarperSanFrancisco, 1994), 47.

2. Ibid., 46–68.

11

JESUS THE PROPHET

Many and varied are the interpretations dealing with the teaching and life of Jesus of Nazareth. But few of these interpretations deal with what the teachings and the life of Jesus have to say to those who stand, at a moment in human history, with their backs against the wall. To those who need profound succor and strength to enable them to live in the present with dignity and creativity, Christianity often has been sterile and of little avail. The conventional Christian word is muffled, confused, and vague. —Howard Thurman[1]

Jesus was more than a prophet, but a prophet he was. He preached a gospel that was good news to the poor, to those with their backs against the wall.

When Jesus rode into Jerusalem on a donkey that final week before the crucifixion, people asked, "Who is this?" The crowds answered, "This is the prophet Jesus from Nazareth of Galilee" (Matthew 21:11). They were not wrong. And it was not the first time Jesus was called "prophet."

Some of Herod's court thought Jesus was a "prophet, like one of the prophets of old" (Mark 6:15). The disciples reported to Jesus that many of that time thought that Jesus was a prophet (Matthew 16:14; Mark 8:28; Luke 9:19). When a "woman of the city" anointed Jesus in the house of Simon the Pharisee, Simon said, "If this man were a prophet, he would have known who and what sort of woman this is who is touching him, for she is a sinner" (Luke 7:39). In Jesus' last week, the high priests and Pharisees were afraid of arresting Jesus because they feared the multitudes, which "held him to be a prophet" (Matthew 21:46). In John's Gospel, the Samaritan woman thinks that Jesus is a prophet because he knows her marital history (John 4:19). Later in John, Jesus' credentials as a prophet are questioned because he is from Galilee (John 7:52). In the Emmaus story in Luke, Jesus is described by two followers as a "prophet mighty in deed and word" (Luke 24:19).

Many Christians today downplay Jesus' role as a prophet because they deny the importance of social justice as part of the Christian mission and message. Even the phrase "social justice" is suspect for such skeptics. It is important, then, to reflect on Jesus' prophet-ness and what that meant. It meant that justice was important as part of the kingdom of God drawn near, and it meant that Jesus addressed the sociopolitical crises of his days.

THE PROPHET AND JUSTICE

The Hebrew Scripture had two words for "prophet." The first meant "seer," one who sees visions and sees reality at its most real. The second word was *nabi*, which means "one who is called." The Hebrew prophet was one who was given visions by God and sought to apply those visions to the realm of "plain history, real politics and human instrumentality."[2] It was not too late!

The prophet challenged people to return to God and live by God's way, the Torah. The prophet was not so much a fore-teller as a forth-teller. The prophet spoke forth God's word, using not a crystal ball but a megaphone. The prophet sometimes warned of coming destruction unless the people turn, repent, and walk in the way of God. The Lord's prophet showed up, as the cowboy poet Buck Ramsey put it, "just before beyond redemption."[3]

The prophet was a prophet of the justice and compassion of God. Micah summarized the desires of God: "What does the LORD require of you but to do justice, and to love kindness, and to walk humbly with your God?" (Micah 6:8).

For the Hebrew prophets, justice and righteousness were twin virtues. The prophet Amos thundered, "Let justice roll down like waters, and righteousness like an ever-flowing stream" (Amos 5:24).

Justice included fairness in the courts and honesty in the marketplace. It defended the poor and the vulnerable. God's justice and righteousness were coming to save them. Righteousness meant right relationship with God and neighbor. And yet, justice and righteousness were more than noble ethical ideals; they were the divine energy, the power of God flowing into the world to transform it.

The Greek idea of justice was captured by Plato's phrase "to every one his *due*." Everyone deserves what he or she has earned. The Hebrew idea of justice was "to every one according to his or her *need*." Biblical demands for justice kept an eye out for the "orphan, widow, and stranger," the most vulnerable of society. A constant drumbeat in the Hebrew Scriptures is the command to care for the widow, the orphan, and the stranger (see Deuteronomy 14:28-29; Psalm 146:9; Jeremiah 7:5-7).

Similarly, in Jesus' parable of the last judgment, Jesus said that the nations and peoples will be judged by how they care for the hungry, thirsty, stranger, naked, sick, and imprisoned, for the "least of these" (Matthew 25:31-46). Indeed, to care for these was to care for Jesus himself, who waits for us in them. And Jesus meant more than acts of charity; he meant a just society too.

In Mark 12:38-40, Jesus warned against the scribes who like the best seats in the synagogue, loved to pray long prayers, yet who "devour widows' houses." He stood against the Roman occupiers and religious leaders who conspired to reward the rich and rob the poor. "Blessed are you poor," Jesus said, "for yours is the kingdom of God"; and, "Woe to you that are rich, for you have received your consolation" (Luke 6:20,24).

In the New Testament the word for "righteousness," *dikaiosynē*, stood for both social justice and personal morality. It stood for God's justice and compassion flowing in the world as the mighty river of Amos. We today hear the word *righteousness* used to mean personal morality and not social justice too. It would be a corrective to add the word *justice* to *righteousness* in some of Jesus' most famous sayings:

> *Blessed are those who hunger and thirst for justice and*
> *righteousness,*
> *for they will be satisfied.*
> *Blessed are those who are persecuted for the sake of justice*
> *and righteousness,*
> *for theirs is the kingdom of heaven.*
> *Unless your justice and righteousness exceed that of the scribes*
> *and Pharisees,*
> *you will never enter the kingdom of heaven.*
> (Matthew 5:6,10,20)

For Jesus, righteousness was the power of God sweeping into history and into our lives. So we can speak of the "justice-ing" and "righteous-ing" power of God. This was the kingdom of God that Jesus preached: the rectifying and healing power of God impinging on the world to transform the world.

Some of Jesus' harshest words were reserved for the scribes and Pharisees because of their neglect of the justice and mercy of God:

> Woe to you scribes and Pharisees, hypocrites! For you tithe
> mint, dill, and cumin, and have neglected the weightier

matters of the law: *justice* and *mercy* and *faith*. . . . You blind guides! You strain out a gnat but swallow a camel! (Matthew 23:23-24, NRSV [emphasis added])

He was echoing Micah's words to do justice, love mercy, and walk humbly with God.

Jesus used comic-book-like exaggeration to make his point: You go to your little herb gardens and snip and weigh and take your tiny tithes to the temple but ignore the really weighty matters of God—justice, mercy, and faith. You take fastidious care to strain a gnat out of your soup, and you end up swallowing a camel! Head first, then teeth and whiskers, the neck, front legs, hump, the back legs, and finally the bristly tail.

In Luke's version, Jesus described the weightier matters of the law as "justice and the love of God" (Luke 11:42), which corresponds to his double commandment as the greatest: love God with all your heart, mind, soul, and strength, and love your neighbor as yourself.

THE PROPHET'S LAST WEEK

Later in his last week, Jesus would engage in two prophetic action signs: the entry into Jerusalem and the cleansing of the temple. Did he think of himself as a prophet? This speech suggests so:

O Jerusalem, Jerusalem, killing the prophets and stoning those who are sent to you! How often would I have gathered your children together as a hen gathers her brood under her wings, and you would not! Behold, your house is forsaken and desolate. (Matthew 23:37-38)

He offered a prophetic lament over Jerusalem, saying, "Would that even today you knew the things that make for peace! But now they are hid from your eyes" (Luke 19:42).

When Jesus cleansed the temple, overturning the tables and driving out the money changers, he said as part of the prophetic action-sign, "Is it not written, 'My house shall be called a house of prayer for all the nations'? But you have made it a den of robbers" (Mark 11:17, NRSV). In that moment, he echoed the prophet Jeremiah in Jeremiah 7:1-11.

Jesus then prophesied the destruction of the temple:

> And as he came out of the temple, one of his disciples said to him, "Look, Teacher, what wonderful stones and what wonderful buildings!" And Jesus said to him, "Do you see these great buildings? There will not be left here one stone upon another; all will be thrown down. (Mark 13:1-2, NRSV)

He was addressing the social crisis facing Israel. The temple was a magnificent building set high on the temple mount, some of the stones weighing seventy tons. Jesus was speaking of a cataclysmic event when Jerusalem would be utterly destroyed. This happened forty years later, in 70 CE, when Rome answered a Jewish uprising with total destruction. Was Jesus thinking also about *God* rebuilding the temple in a new age of justice and peace? Perhaps. Did he see his own life and death as part of God's redemption of the present age? I think so.

As prophet of God, Jesus proclaimed the sole sovereignty of God. The kingdom of God opposed all impostors to divine rule—in Jesus' time, the Roman Empire, whose king-like Caesar was called "son of God" and "savior of the world." Jesus warned his nation of coming destruction. He preached the justice-making power of God against injustice and raised up the poor and weak. In all these ways he was a classical Hebrew prophet.

Jesus was well aware of the tradition of the prophets that led to their deaths. He was acquainted with the songs of the Suffering Servant in the book of Isaiah, which said that God would heal the nation through the suffering of God's servant. He saw the kingdom of God and its justice, compassion, and peace coming through God's anointed one and saw himself as the anointed of God. Trusting in God, he did not take up the sword as others would do in the nascent but fast-growing Zealot movement.

Jesus would give his life and his death in service of God and God's kingdom, trusting himself into the hands of God, who would bring in the kingdom of justice, compassion, and peace in God's own way. Jesus was more than a prophet, but a prophet he was.

The traditions of prophetic Christianity have been kept alive in American Christianity through the progressive wings of Protestant and Catholic faith and through the African American church. Martin Luther King Jr. was an exemplar of prophetic Christianity. Drawing on Hebrew prophets and Jesus the prophet, King led the Civil Rights Movement as a movement to transform American society according to God's dream for the world. He said about the Montgomery bus boycott: "It was Jesus of Nazareth that stirred the Negroes to protest with the creative power of love."[4]

Speaking to his congregation about what he would want people to say at his funeral, King said:

> I'd like somebody to mention that day, that *Martin Luther King, Jr.* tried to give his life serving others. I'd like for somebody to say that day that Martin Luther King, Jr. tried to love somebody. I want you to say that day that I tried to be right on the war question. I want you to be able to say that I *did* try to feed the hungry. . . . I want you to say that I tried to *love* and *serve* humanity. Yes, if you want to say that I was a drum major, *say* that I was a *drum major* for justice. Say that I was a drum major for peace. That I was a drum major for righteousness. All of the other shallow things will not matter.[5]

The life of Jesus the prophet lives on in people committed to his way.

NOTES

1. Howard Thurman, *Jesus and the Disinherited* (Boston: Beacon Press, 1976), 11.

2. Paul Hanson, *The Dawn of Apocalyptic: The Historical and Sociological Roots of Jewish Apocalyptic Theology* (Philadelphia: Fortress Press, 1975), 11–12.

3. Buck Ramsey, "Anthem," *Texas Monthly*, April 2002, http://www.texas monthly.com/articles/anthem/.

4. As cited in Kenneth L. Smith and Ira G. Zepp Jr., *Search for the Beloved Community: The Thinking of Martin Luther King, Jr.* (Valley Forge, PA: Judson Press, 1974), 18.

5. As cited in Stephen B. Oates, *Let the Trumpet Sound: A Life of Martin Luther King, Jr.* (New York: Harper & Row, 1982), 458.

12

JESUS AND NONVIOLENCE

War after war has been prosecuted by bloodthirsty Christians, and to the profit of greedy Christians, as if Christ had never been born and the Gospels never written.

—Wendell Berry[1]

Some of Jesus' most confounding, demanding, admired, and ignored teachings have to do with what has been called "nonviolence," or what we might name "unbounded love."

In Wendell Berry's novel *Jayber Crow*, Jayber has become the town barber rather than his first vocational idea, to be a preacher. Jayber is now living through World War II, with all its horror and loss, alongside his townspeople and neighbors. He says, "I was glad enough that I had not become a preacher, and so would not have to go through a war pretending that Jesus had not told us to love our enemies."[2]

A lot of Christians do a lot of pretending that Jesus did not say, "Love your enemies." We have made substantial compromise with Jesus' teaching, calling it impractical or impossible. Scholars, preachers, and general followers of Jesus have sought to soften the rigor of Jesus' commands and come up with reasons why they don't apply to us. To the evasion that loving our enemies is not practical we might ask: How would we know that it's impractical, given that it has so seldom been practiced? As to the impossibility of Jesus' commands, he himself had an answer: "For mortals it is impossible, but for God all things are possible" (Matthew 19:26, NRSV).

It may be profitable simply to read some of Jesus' sayings and let them cause us to reflect on the ways of Jesus.

> Blessed are the meek (gentle),
> for they will inherit the earth.
> Blessed are those who hunger and thirst for righteousness,
> for they will be filled.
> Blessed are the merciful,
> for they will receive mercy. . . .
> Blessed are the peacemakers,
> for they will be called children of God.
> (Matthew 5:5-7,9, NRSV)

> You have heard that it was said to those of ancient times, "You shall not murder"; and "whoever murders shall be liable to judgment." But I say to you that if you are angry with a brother or sister, you will be liable to judgment. (Matthew 5:21-22, NRSV)

> You have heard it was said, "An eye for an eye and a tooth for a tooth." But I say to you, Do not resist an evildoer. But if anyone strikes you on the right cheek, turn the other also. (Matthew 5:38-39, NRSV)

> You have heard that it was said, "You shall love your neighbor and hate your enemy." But I say to you, Love your enemies and pray for those who persecute you, so that you may be children of your Father in heaven; for God makes his sun rise on the evil and on the good, and sends rain on the righteous and unrighteous. . . . Be perfect, therefore, as your heavenly Father is perfect. (Matthew 5:43-45,48, NRSV [adapted])

In everything do to others as you would have them do to you; for this is the law and the prophets. (Matthew 7:12, NRSV)

See, I am sending you out like sheep into the midst of wolves; so be wise as serpents and innocent as doves. (Matthew 10:16, NRSV)

So it is not the will of my Father who is in heaven that one of these little ones should perish. (Matthew 18:14)

"Teacher, which commandment in the law is the greatest?" He said to him, "'You shall love the Lord your God with all your heart, and with all your soul, and with all your mind.' This is the greatest and the first commandment. And a second is like it: 'You shall love your neighbor as yourself.' On these two commandments hang all the law and the prophets." (Matthew 22:36-40, NRSV)

Then they came and laid hands on Jesus and arrested him. Suddenly, one of those with Jesus put his hand on his sword, drew it, and struck the slave of the high priest, cutting off his ear. Then Jesus said to him, "Put your sword back into its place; for all those who take the sword will perish by the sword." (Matthew 26:50-52, NRSV)

But love your enemies, do good, and lend, expecting nothing in return. Your reward will be great, and you will be children of the Most High; for God is kind to the ungrateful and the wicked. Be merciful, just as your Father is merciful. (Luke 6:35-36, NRSV [adapted])

When the days drew near for him to be taken up, he set his face to go to Jerusalem. And he sent messengers ahead of him. On their way they entered a village of the Samaritans to make ready for him; but they did not receive him,

> because his face was set toward Jerusalem. When his disciples James and John saw it, they said, "Lord, do you want us to command fire to come down from heaven and consume them?" But he turned and rebuked them. (Luke 9:51-55, NRSV) [No wonder Jesus called James and John "sons of thunder"!]

> Then Pilate entered the headquarters again, summoned Jesus, and asked him, "Are you the king of the Jews?" . . . Jesus answered, "My kingdom is not from this world. If my kingdom were from this world, my followers would be fighting to keep me from being handed over to the Jews." (John 18:33,36, NRSV)

Mark Twain once said, "It ain't those parts of the Bible that I can't understand that bother me, it's the parts that I *do* understand!"

The plain sense of Jesus' teaching confronts us. Did he not teach nonviolence? There are authors new and old who have tried to paint Jesus as a Zealot, a violent resister of the Roman occupation. They argue that the Gospel writers wanting to escape Roman persecution created a pacifist Jesus and downplayed his more incendiary sayings. Reza Aslan, author of *Zealot: The Life and Times of Jesus of Nazareth*, is the most recent.[3] S. G. F. Brandon, in *Jesus and the Zealots*, made this case in the 1960s.[4] They make one saying of Jesus their centerpiece:

> Do not think that I have come to bring peace to the earth; I have not come to bring peace, but a sword. (Matthew 10:34, NRSV)

But the meaning of this saying is that Jesus' coming has brought divisions among people, even among families (see Matthew 10:35-37).

To choose a few sayings out of the hundreds of Jesus in the Gospel and use them to overturn the meaning of the rest of Jesus' teaching is a dubious enterprise. The case for Jesus as a Zealot (the Zealots as a major party did not arise until around 60 CE) is further eroded by two historical circumstances.

The first is that he did not resist his arrest and conviction. Indeed on the cross, Jesus prayed for his enemies, as he himself taught, and cried, "Father, forgive them for they know not what they do" (Luke 23:34). Second, and furthermore, as John Dominic Crossan points out, the Romans did not go after Jesus' disciples to kill them. Had they thought Jesus was mounting an armed revolt, they would have done so.

Jesus' way of nonviolence has inspired people throughout the centuries, including Mahatma Gandhi, Leo Tolstoy, and Martin Luther King Jr. We can oppose the powers of evil, but as followers of Jesus, we must do so nonviolently.

We can try to "interpret" or "explain" Jesus' teaching in ways that lessen their demand on those who follow him, but we can't go around pretending that Jesus did not tell us to love our enemies.

NOTES

1. Wendell Berry, *Blessed Are the Peacemakers: Christ's Teachings about Love, Compassion, and Forgiveness* (Emeryville, CA: Shoemaker & Hoard, 2005), 4.

2. Wendell Berry, *Jayber Crow: A Novel* (Washington, DC: Counterpoint, 2000), 142.

3. Reza Aslan, *Zealot: The Life and Times of Jesus of Nazareth* (New York: Random House, 2013).

4. S. G. F. Brandon, *Jesus and the Zealots: A Study of the Political Faction in Primitive Christianity* (New York: Scribner, 1967).

13

JESUS THE TEACHER, THE SAGE, THE WISDOM OF GOD

Jesus was a teacher of striking authority. He interpreted the Torah; he taught wisdom; he himself was the Wisdom of God. This chapter will explore all three dimensions.

JESUS AS INTERPRETER OF TORAH

As every good rabbi would do, Jesus helped people read and interpret Torah, the first five books of the Hebrew Bible, also called the Law of Moses, and the heart of the Jewish way of life. Jesus interpreted Torah in light of the in-breaking kingdom of God. It was a new way of interpreting Torah, which appeared to some critics to be a jettisoning of it, but Jesus answered, "Do not think that I have come to abolish the law or the prophets; I have come not to abolish but to fulfill" (Matthew 5:17, NRSV).

If you want to see Jesus' teaching in summary form, read Matthew 5–7, which we know as the Sermon on the Mount. It became a kind of manual for new converts to Christianity in the early church.

Six times in the Sermon on the Mount Jesus said with breathtaking authority, "You have heard it said of old, but I say unto you. . . ."

He deepened "Thou shalt not murder" to a prohibition of anger. He deepened "no adultery" to "no lust." He made stricter the conditions of divorce. He deepened "no false swearing" to "no swearing." He deepened "an eye for an eye" into nonretaliation. And he extended love of neighbor to include love of enemy (Matthew 5:21-48).

In Matthew 6 Jesus taught the true way of prayer and piety (6:1-18). He taught a right relationship with riches (6:19-24), and he taught a way to live without worry, trusting in the provision of our Father in heaven, who loves us (6:25-34).

Jesus taught, "Judge not, that you be not judged" (Matthew 7:1), and the Golden Rule: "In everything do to others as you would have them do to you" (Matthew 7:12, NRSV). He warned his followers to enter by the narrow gate:

> Enter by the narrow gate; for the gate is wide and the way is easy, that leads to destruction, and those who enter by it are many. For the gate is narrow and the way is hard, that leads to life, and those who find it are few. (Matthew 7:13-14)

In his poem, "To the Holy Spirit," Wendell Berry intones, "By Thy wide grace show me Thy narrow gate."[1]

JESUS AS WISDOM TEACHER

According to a category that biblical scholars are using more today, Jesus was a "wisdom" teacher, a sage, but not just any kind of sage. New Testament scholar Ben Witherington describes him as "a prophetic sage offering primarily counter-order wisdom."[2] In this way, Jesus not only fulfilled the sections of Hebrew Scripture known as the Law (Torah) and the Prophets, but also the Writings, which includes wisdom books such as Psalms, Proverbs, Job, and Ecclesiastes.

Traditional proverbs convey conventional wisdom. The biblical book of Proverbs is full of them:

> Those who guard their mouths preserve their lives;
> those who open wide their lips come to ruin.
> (Proverbs 13:3, NRSV)

> A slack hand brings poverty,
> but the hand of the diligent makes rich.
> (Proverbs 10:4)

> A cheerful heart is a good medicine,
> but a downcast spirit dries up the bones.
> (Proverbs 17:22)

Jesus majored not in conventional wisdom, but in "counterorder" wisdom, the transformational wisdom of the inbreaking kingdom of God. Jesus offered aphorisms rather than proverbs. Witherington explains the contrast, clarifying that "a proverb is a short sentence founded on long experience containing a truth. . . . Aphorisms by contrast provide not the wisdom of a collective group . . . but rather the unique insight of a creative individual."[3]

Here are some of Jesus' aphorisms:

> "So the last will be first, and the first last." (Matthew 20:16)

> "For those who want to save their life will lose it, and those who lose their life for my sake, and for the sake of the gospel, will save it." (Mark 8:35, NRSV)

> "It is easier for a camel to go through the eye of a needle than for someone who is rich to enter the kingdom of God." (Mark 10:25, NRSV)

> "Why do you see the speck in your neighbor's eye, but do not notice the log in your own eye?" (Matthew 7:3, NRSV)

"No one can serve two masters. . . . You cannot serve God and wealth." (Matthew 6:24, NRSV)

Here was a "counter-order" wisdom. For example, in Psalms and Proverbs, prosperity was a sign of God's blessing on your righteousness. In Jesus' aphorisms, wealth is an obstacle to entering the kingdom of God. Jesus came preaching the radical way of the kingdom and used surprisingly inventive aphorisms to make his point.

JESUS AS THE DIVINE WISDOM

But is there more afoot? Was Jesus more than a teacher of wisdom? Was he himself the Wisdom of God made flesh? Did he see himself this way? Did others?

John's Gospel begins with a theological poem that could be translated this way if we substitute the Hebrew word *hokmah*, "wisdom," for the Greek word *logos*, "word":

In the beginning was Wisdom.
And Wisdom was with God and was God.
Wisdom was in the beginning with God.
All things were made through Wisdom,
and without Wisdom was not anything made that was made.
In Wisdom was life,
and the life was the light of humanity. . . .
And Wisdom became flesh and dwelt among us . . .
full of grace and truth.
(John 1:1-4,14, [adapted])

Here is a startling theological move. Jesus is the divine Wisdom, or Sophia, made flesh. (*Sophia* is the Greek word used to translate *hokmah* in the Septuagint, the Greek translation of the Hebrew Scriptures.) In the book of Proverbs, we see *hokmah* personified in the feminine as the daughter, or darling child, of God. In Proverbs 8, Daughter Wisdom sings:

Before the mountains had been shaped,
    before the hills, I was brought forth—
when he had not yet made earth and fields,
    or the world's first bits of soil.
When he established the heavens, I was there,
    when he drew a circle on the face of the deep . . .
    then I was beside him like a master worker;
and I was daily his delight,
    rejoicing before him always,
rejoicing in his inhabited world
    and delighting in the human race.
(Proverbs 8:25-31, NRSV)

Who is Jesus as the wisdom of God? Theologian Paul Vallieri writes, "Christ as Sophia is the humanity which God sees and loves from all eternity."[4] Sophia is the kindness and mercy of God now made flesh in Jesus. Sophia is the presence of God in all creation whose way is peace. Famed monastic Thomas Merton wrote, "There is in all things an invisible fecundity . . . a hidden wholeness. This mysterious Unity and Integrity is Wisdom, the Mother of all."[5]

The apostle Paul envisioned Jesus as the Wisdom of God in his christological hymn in Colossians:

> He is the image of the invisible God, the firstborn of all creation; for in him all things in heaven and on earth were created. . . all things have been created through him and for him. . . . For in him all the fullness of God was placed to dwell, and through him God was pleased to reconcile to himself all things, whether on earth or in heaven, by making peace through the blood of his cross. (Colossians 1:15-20, NRSV)

Did Jesus see himself as the Wisdom of God made manifest? One of his most beloved sayings goes:

Come to me, all who labor and are heavy laden, and I will give you rest. Take up my yoke upon you, and learn from me; for I am gentle and lowly in heart, and you will find rest for your souls. For my yoke is easy, and my burden is light. (Matthew 11:28-30)

Compare these words with these from Sirach (Ecclesiasticus), a wisdom book written between the time of the Old Testament and that of the New Testament:

Come to her like one who plows and sows,
    and wait for her good harvest. . . .
Put your feet into her fetters,
    and your neck into her collar. . . .
Come to her with all your soul,
    and keep her ways with all your might. . . .
And when you get hold of her,
    do not let her go.
For at last you will find the rest she gives,
    and she will be changed into joy for you.
Then her fetters will become to you a strong defense,
    and her collar a glorious robe.
(Sirach 6:19,24-29, NRSV)

Did Jesus see himself not just as a teacher of wisdom, but Wisdom herself? His words in Matthew 11 suggest as much, and the early church certainly thought so. Contemporary explorations of Jesus as the Wisdom, *Hokmah*, Sophia of God are an exciting new venture in theology in general and in Christology particularly. Such work is providing a bridge to feminist and environmental theologies and to interfaith dialogue. Think of it: Jesus is the prism of the pure light of God's wisdom given to all people since the beginning of the world. He is God's love for all people and for creation itself.

If Jesus was the Wisdom of God, parables were his tongue. As Matthew's Gospel reports, "Indeed he said nothing to them without a parable. This was to fulfil what was spoken by the prophet: 'I will open my mouth in parables, I will utter what has been hidden since the foundation of the world'" (Matthew 13:34-35). Later in that same chapter, Jesus said, "Therefore every scribe who has been trained for the kingdom of heaven is like a householder who brings out of his treasure what is new and what is old" (Matthew 13:52). There is something ancient and something new in the teaching of Jesus. He embodied the primordial wisdom of God and made it urgently present for his listeners.

To Jesus and his parables we now turn.

NOTES

1. Wendell Berry, "To the Holy Spirit," in Wendell Berry, *Collected Poems, 1957–1982* (San Francisco: North Point Press, 1984), 209.

2. Ben Witherington III, *Jesus the Sage: The Pilgrimage of Wisdom* (Minneapolis: Fortress Press, 2000), 385.

3. Ibid., 9.

4. As cited in Christopher Pramuk, *Sophia: The Hidden Christ of Thomas Merton* (Collegeville, MN: Liturgical Press, 2009), 219.

5. Thomas Merton, "Hagia Sophia," as quoted in Pramuk, *Sophia*, 301. In this book, Pramuk examines Sophia as the central motif of Merton's theology and traces the influence of Russian theologians Vladimir Soloviev and Sergei Bulgakov and their "sophiologies."

14

JESUS AND HIS PARABLES

The main subject of Jesus' teaching was the kingdom of God. And the main way he taught about it was in parables.

Think of our world as one circle and the kingdom of God as another. Jesus said that by the grace of God the circles overlap. The kingdom of God is "at hand," or within you, among you, in your midst—"*entos* you" (Luke 17:21). Jesus' parables illustrate the area where the circles overlap. They help us imagine what the kingdom of God is like—and to imagine our lives as part of it.

"Parable" is the English translation of the Hebrew word *mashal*, which stood for a variety of figurative speech, from proverbs and aphorisms to riddles to parables. Jesus' parables were "narrative *mashalim*."[1] The Greek word for "parable" (*parabole*) means literally "to throw alongside." Jesus' parables threw the kingdom of God alongside our everyday lives and invited us to enter the kingdom of God with its compassion, joy, and startling grace.

One New Testament scholar describes Jesus' parables as "short narrative fictions that serve as metaphors."[2] Metaphors bring together two things not usually brought together, and in so doing they make something new happen in our minds and hearts. The more surprising the juxtaposition, the

more powerful the metaphor: God our mother, Jesus the misfit, Pilate the fly.

"The kingdom of God is like . . . ," Jesus said again and
again, and then he would launch into one of his parables.

The kingdom is like a big party that a king threw and invited all the bigwigs, the VIPs. But they all made excuses and
said no. So the king told his servants to go out into the city
streets, the highways and the byways, and invite anybody,
everybody to the party (Matthew 22:1-14; Luke 14:15-24).

The kingdom is like finding and being found. A woman
lost a precious coin and turned her house upside down to
find it, and when she did, she invited all the neighbors to her
house for a party (Luke 15:8-10).

Most parables had this strategy: Jesus would invite us into
our familiar workaday world, the world as we know and
experience it. We would climb inside the story. Then there
would come a surprise that turned the familiar world upside
down, inside out, right side up.

In Matthew 20:1-16, a group of day laborers was recruited
for work at 6:00 a.m. The boss promised a fair day's wage, a
denarius. They happily agreed and set to work. Another group
was hired at 9:00 a.m., another at noon, another at 3:00 p.m.,
and a final one at 5:00 p.m., with only one more hour left to
work. When the boss came to pay the workers, he started with
the ones hired last and paid them a denarius, a full day's pay
for one hour's work. Those hired first, who had worked all day
in the hot sun, were incensed. "No fair!" they exclaimed. A literal translation of the boss's response in verse 15 is: "Is your
eye evil because I am good? Do you begrudge my generosity?"

The parable gets under our skin. We want things to be fair;
we feel aggrieved, like those hired first who worked all day.
But at the end of the day, at the end of our lives, would you
rather God be fair or be generous? Will you begrudge God's
mercy to others, or will you laugh at the beauty of it all?

Jesus' parables aimed for the heart. A shepherd left the
ninety-nine sheep to go after the one who was lost (Luke

15:3-7). Are you among the ninety-nine safely in the fold, or are you the one who is lost? Are you happy with the sight of the shepherd carrying the lost sheep home?

In Jesus' parables there is almost always the element of surprise. Look for the surprise. The kingdom of God is surprise. Consider these twin parables, related in rapid succession:

> The kingdom of heaven is like a treasure hidden in a field, which a man found and covered up; then in his joy he goes and sells all that he has and buys that field. Again the kingdom of heaven is like a merchant in search of fine pearls, who, on finding one pearl of great value, went and sold all that he had and bought it. (Matthew 13:44-46)

In the first parable, the tenant farmer was not looking for a treasure but unexpectedly found it and "in his joy" sold all that he had to buy the field so he could own the treasure. The kingdom is joy. In the second parable, the pearl merchant was searching for pearls but unexpectedly found the pearl of his dreams, and he sold all that he owned, all the other pearls, to have this one. The kingdom is the treasure that costs us everything, but our everything is small in comparison to the surpassing worth of the treasure. Together, these parables declare that the kingdom is worth everything. We do not know this, however, until we find it or it finds us.

Jesus' two most famous parables are in Luke's Gospel, and they have stirred the imagination of people for two thousand years, both Christian and non-Christian.

The first is the parable of the good Samaritan, although that title robs us of the surprise ending (Luke 10:29-37). A man fell among thieves who robbed him, beat him, and left him on the road to die. A priest came by and passed on without helping the man. A Levite came along, and he too passed by without helping. Then came a Samaritan, a man despised by the Jews. He stopped, dressed the man's wounds, and carried him on his donkey to an inn, where he nursed him through the night. The next morning the Samaritan paid for the room and gave the innkeeper his credit card and said, "Take care of him and charge it to me."

The story was told to answer the question "Who is my neighbor?" Jesus stretches our moral imagination. Our neighbor is anyone in need. The kingdom is a community of neighbors. And there's the scandal of a hated Samaritan who becomes the hero with his risky, extravagant compassion. Jesus is changing us from enemies to friends. This story has touched people for centuries and generations.

The parable of the prodigal son is the second famous parable in Luke (see Luke 15:11-32). Actually, the story is about *two* sons lost in their own different ways. The younger son asked his father for his share of the inheritance while the father still lived, a request of shameful disrespect. The father gave it to him and so probably was seen by the villagers as an old fool.

The young man went to the "far country," where he wasted his inheritance through "loose living." Desperate, he sold himself to a pig farmer to work feeding pigs—degradation for a Jewish boy raised to view pigs as unclean.

Then came the moment of "turning." The young man "came to himself" and returned home carefully rehearsing his speech of repentance: "Father, I have sinned against heaven and before you; I am no longer worth to be called your son; treat me as one of your hired servants" (Luke 15:19, NRSV).

When the son reached the edge of the village, his father saw him from a distance, had compassion on him, and, running, embraced and kissed his son. In front of the whole startled village, the father ran and welcomed his son home.

The son started his speech of repentance, but before he could finish, the father said to his servants:

> "Bring quickly the best robe, and put it on him; and put a ring on his hand, and shoes on his feet; [the robe, the ring, the shoes of restored sonship] and bring the fatted calf and

kill it, and let us eat and make merry; for this my son was dead, and is alive again; he was lost, and is found." And they began to make merry. (Luke 15:22-23)

But all is not well. When the older brother heard the party going on and discovered for whom it was given, he grew angry and refused to go in—a rebuke to his brother, an insult to his father.

The father "went out," this time for his older son. The son spewed his anger: "I've worked like a dog, like a slave for you all these years, and you've never thrown a party for me and my friends. But here this 'son of yours' has devoured your living with whores, and you kill for him the fatted calf!"

The father lovingly, patiently pled with his son: "Son, you are always with me, and all that is mine is yours. It was fitting to make merry and be glad, for this your brother was dead, and is alive; he was lost, and is found" (Luke 15:31-32).

It is the sublime story of a father's love for both sons, though the elder son will not accept it, but only stews in the juices of his self-righteousness and envy.

Who are we in this story? It strikes the heart as we enter it and identify with one or more of the characters. The story is emblazoned on the collective consciousness of the world. It has been turned into art, literature, and song. It is, above all, the story of the extravagant, never-giving-up love of God for us and of God's joy at our return to self and to God.

This story was told to answer the grumbling of the righteous folk who criticized Jesus' dinner parties with sinners and his welcome of all people into the kingdom of God. It is to this dimension of his ministry that we now turn.

NOTES

1. Ben Witherington III, *Jesus the Sage: The Pilgrimage of Wisdom* (Minneapolis: Fortress Press, 2000), 183–201.

2. Bernard Brandon Scott, *Re-imagine the World: An Introduction to the Parables of Jesus* (Santa Rosa, CA: Polebridge Press, 2001), 13.

15

JESUS, THE SINNERS, THE POOR, AND THE LITTLE ONES

Jesus came not only for the sick, those distressed of body, mind, and spirit. He came also for the sinners, the poor, and the little ones. He came first for "the lost sheep of the house of Israel" (Matthew 10:6), then for lost sheep everywhere. It was scandal: "Behold, a glutton and a drunkard, a friend of tax collectors and sinners!" (Luke 7:34). Luke reported, "Now the tax collectors and sinners were all drawing near to hear him. The Pharisees and the scribes murmured, saying, 'This man receives sinners and eats with them'" (Luke 15:1-2).

There have been murmurs ever since, the church taking up the role of scribes and Pharisees. Novelist Reynolds Price comments:

> Orthodox Christianity, the church in most its past and present forms, has defaced and even reversed whole broad aspects of Jesus' teaching; but in no case has the church turned more culpably from his aim and his practice than its hateful rejection of what it sees as outcasts: the whores and cheats, the traitors and killers, the baffled and stunned,

the social outlaw, the maimed and hideous and contagious. If it is possible to discern in the gospel documents . . . a conscious goal that sent the man Jesus—himself an urgent function of the Maker of all—to his agonized death, can we detect a surer aim than his first and last announced intent to sweep the lost with him into God's coming reign?[1]

It was of great offense that Jesus befriended sinners. He ate and drank with them—and did not hold his nose.

JESUS AND THE SINNERS

Who were the "sinners"? They were what the Hebrew Scriptures called the *reshaim*, the wicked, those sinners who had no thought of repenting. They included the poor, who could not afford the official channels of repentance, the Jewish sacrificial system. They included tax collectors and prostitutes, whose professions rendered them sinners. New Testament scholar E. P. Sanders writes, "He counted within his fellowship people who were generally living outside the law in a blatant manner."[2]

If Jesus' behavior was scandalous, even more so were his words to the righteous: "Truly, I say to you, the tax collectors and the harlots go into the kingdom of God before you" (Matthew 21:31).

We can imagine their shocked faces. That Jesus had dinner parties with tax collectors and sinners upset the moral and social equilibrium of the culture. Meals normally were the place where the strictest moral and social codes were enforced. Jesus upset them. His meals demonstrated what John Dominic Crossan names "open commensality" and "radical egalitarianism."[3] *All* were invited. Social, religious, and moral boundaries came down. Jesus offered a "politics of compassion" rather than the prevailing "politics of holiness."[4] The kingdom Jesus preached was a "brokerless kingdom"[5] where people without the aid of a hierarchy of priests could have direct access to the mercy of God. "Free healings" and "open meals" were a sign of the kingdom's presence.[6]

To be sure, Jesus called everyone to change, sinners and righteous alike. It was the change *God* wanted and they needed, change measured by the way of the kingdom, not by religious institutions or cultural mores. To some Jesus said, "Change and become as a child." To another he said, "Sell all you have and give to the poor." To Levi the tax collector he said, "Leave your tax office and follow me."

But with Jesus, a fundamental shift was taking place: grace came first, bringing repentance in its healing wings. New Testament scholar Günther Bornkamm wrote, "Salvation and repentance have . . . changed places. . . . So little is repentance a human action preparing the way of grace, that it can be placed on the same level as being found."[7]

Here is the shift from John the Baptizer to Jesus. For John, repentance always came first. For Jesus, grace led the way. Such grace is captured in an eighteenth-century hymn:

Come ye weary, heavy laden,
Lost and ruined by the fall;
If you tarry till you're better,
You will never come at all.[8]

Biblical scholar Joachim Jeremias wrote, "Because repentance means being able to live from forgiveness, being able to be a child again, repentance is joy."[9]

Jesus discovered that sinners were closer to responding to grace and to a true repentance than were the righteous. So Jesus told this parable:

> Two men went up into the temple to pray, one a Pharisee and the other a tax collector. The Pharisee stood and prayed thus with himself: "God, I thank thee that I am not like other men, extortioners, unjust, adulterers, or even

like this tax collector. I fast twice a week, I give tithes of all that I get." But the tax collector, standing far off, would not even lift his eyes to heaven, but beat his breast, saying, "God, be merciful to me a sinner!" I tell you this man went down to his house justified rather than the other; for all who exalt themselves will be humbled, but all who humble themselves will be exalted. (Luke 18:10-14 adapted)

JESUS, THE POOR, AND THE *NĒPIOI*

Jesus came not only for the sinners, but also for the poor, the *am haarets* (people of the land), the uneducated, the disinherited, those trapped in the oppressive conditions of Roman-occupied Palestine in that day, those with their "backs against the wall" (to recall Howard Thurman's description). Imagine their shining faces when Jesus said, "Blessed are you poor, for yours is the kingdom of God" (Luke 6:20).

Jesus came for the *nēpioi*, the "little ones," sometimes translated as "babes" or "infants." But *nēpioi* stood for a larger designation of people: those of little notice, little rank, the marginalized, the sick, women and children. To them, Jesus' beatitudes would have sounded like the best news they had ever heard:

Blessed are the poor in spirit,
    for theirs is the kingdom of the heavens.
Blessed are those who mourn,
    for they shall be comforted.
Blessed are the gentle,
    for they shall inherit the earth.
Blessed are those who thirst for justice and righteousness,
    for they shall be satisfied.
Blesses are the merciful,
    for they shall receive mercy.
Blessed are the pure in heart,
    for they shall see God.

> *Blessed are the peacemakers,*
>   *for they shall be called children of God.*
> (Matthew 5:3-9 adapted)

Jesus said of the *nēpioi*, "See that you do not despise one of these little ones; for I tell you that in heaven their angels always behold the face of my Father who is in heaven" (Matthew 18:10).

The *nēpioi* were those whom Jesus called "the least of these." In his parable of the last judgment Jesus said that those who would inherit the joy of the kingdom were those who cared for (note the specificity) *the hungry, the thirsty, the stranger* (immigrant), *the naked, the sick, the imprisoned.* And he said that what we did for them, we did for *him* (see Matthew 25:31-46).

There was a moment in Jesus' ministry when he recognized that the tide had turned against him, that he was being rejected by the wise and powerful and accepted by the little ones. In the face of this crisis, he prayed: "I thank you, *Abba*, God of heaven and earth, because you have hidden these things from the wise and learned and revealed them to the little ones [*nēpioi*]. Yes, *Abba*, for such was your gracious will" (Matthew 11:25-26 [my translation]). He had come for the "little ones," and they alone had responded.

One story in particular highlights Jesus' ministry to the sinners and outcasts (see Luke 19:1-10). Jesus was entering Jericho where a man named Zacchaeus lived. Zacchaeus was doubly damned, being a tax collector who had become very rich. He had exploited people for financial gain. He heard that Jesus was coming to town. Being short, he could not see over the crowd. Becoming as a child, he scampered up a sycamore tree to see Jesus passing along.

Jesus stopped when he got to the tree and said, "Zacchaeus, hurry down from that tree, for I must stay at your house today." The crowd was not happy. "He has gone in to be the guest of a man who is a sinner," they murmured.

Zacchaeus "received Jesus joyfully" into his home, and during the meal he stood and said to Jesus, "Look, half of my possessions, Lord, I will give to the poor; and if I have defrauded anyone of anything, I will pay back four times as much" (Luke 19:8, NRSV).

His servants probably fainted on the spot. Zacchaeus had just gone way beyond what the law required for repentance and restitution. The divine friendship had worked its grace and brought repentance. Walter Rauschenbusch, the father of the social gospel movement in America, wrote of that moment, "Here a camel passed through the eye of a needle and Jesus stood and cheered."[10] What Jesus said was, "Today, salvation has come to this house. . . . For the Son of Man came to seek and to save the lost" (Luke 19:9-10).

The least, the last, and the lost; the sinners, the sick, and the sad; the poor, the disinherited, and the little ones—to them, for them, Jesus came. And still he comes for them. And still there is offense.

NOTES

1. Reynolds Price, *The Three Gospels* (New York: Scribner, 1996), 33.

2. E. P. Sanders, *The Historical Figure of Jesus* (New York: Penguin Books, 1993), 227.

3. John Dominic Crossan, *Jesus: A Revolutionary Biography* (San Francisco: HarperSanFrancisco, 1989), 66–74.

4. Marcus Borg, *Meeting Jesus Again for the First Time: The Historical Jesus and the Heart of Contemporary Faith* (San Francisco: HarperSanFrancisco, 1994), 46–68.

5. John Dominic Crossan, *The Historical Jesus: The Life of a Mediterranean Jewish Peasant* (San Francisco: HarperSanFrancisco, 1991), 422.

6. Ibid.

7. Günther Bornkamm, *Jesus of Nazareth*, trans. Irene and Fraser McLuskey with James M. Robinson (New York: Harper, 1960), 83–84.

8. Joseph Hart, "Come, Ye Sinners, Poor and Needy" (1759).

9. Joachim Jeremias, *New Testament Theology: The Proclamation of Jesus* (New York: Scribner, 1971), 158. See also Albert Nolan's excellent description of the poor in *Jesus before Christianity* (Maryknoll, NY: Orbis Books, 1970), 27–36.

10. Walter Rauschenbusch, *The Social Principles of Jesus* (New York: Association Press, 1921), 68.

16

JESUS AND THE CHILDREN

Prominently among the *nēpioi*, "little ones," were children. Through the centuries, theologians and New Testament scholars have given scant attention to Jesus' relationship with children. (Women scholars are changing that.)[1] But go into children's Sunday school classrooms and look at pictures on the wall, thumb through illustrated Bibles, go into cathedrals and look at the stained glass windows. Prominent among the scenes depicted of Jesus' ministry is one with Jesus with children gathered around, often with a child in his arms. The people's theology is closer to the Gospels than is the professionals' theology.

CHILDREN AND JESUS

We begin with the scene from Mark, repeated in Matthew and Luke—the Gospel writers knew its importance. It pictures Jesus bringing children into his arms to bless them. Novelist Mary Gordon remarks that Jesus is unique in ancient literature as an "affectionate hero." He seemed to want the presence of children, want their company, she says.[2]

In Mark's iconic text, we read, "People were bringing little children to him in order that he might touch them" (Mark 10:13, NRSV)—touch them to bless and to heal.

It is surprising how many of Jesus' healings were of children. He healed a child with epilepsy (Matthew 17:14-21; Mark 9:14-29; Luke 9:37-43). He healed the daughter of Jairus, leader of a synagogue (Matthew 9:18-26; Mark 5:21-43; Luke 8:40-56). He healed the daughter of a Canaanite woman, albeit only after some testy conversation with the mother (Matthew 15:21-28; Mark 7:24-30). He healed the son of a Roman official in Capernaum (John 4:46-54).

Did you catch the amazing mix of people whose children he healed? Who they were in status, race, religion, nationality did not matter. He healed solely out of their need and out of the compassion of God. God's healing transcends our categories of deserving or undeserving. In God's kingdom, we "haven't to deserve," to use the words of poet Robert Frost.[3]

So parents and grandparents were bringing their children to be blessed and healed. The disciples, however, did not think that Jesus had time for such. The kingdom was at hand! They had a lot to do. Jesus had a lot to do. They were on their way to Jerusalem. So they tried to shoo the children away.

Jesus would not have it. He grew "indignant," the text says, which means, as one put it, some "serious disapproval." Sometimes Jesus seriously disapproves! Jesus said, "Let the little children come to me; do not stop them" (Mark 10:14, NRSV). For the umpteenth time in the Gospels, the disciples had egg on their faces.

Then Jesus said, "For it is to such as these that the kingdom of God belongs" (Mark 10:14, NRSV). To such as these belongs the kingdom, he said; and if to them, I think, maybe even to me!

Then Jesus added a saying, which (in one form or another) is in all the Gospels: "Truly I tell you, whoever does not receive the kingdom of God as a little child will never enter it" (Mark 10:15, NRSV). *Never enter it.* In Matthew he put the point more sharply: "Unless you change (*change!*) and become like children, you will never enter the kingdom of heaven" (Matthew 18:3, NRSV). In John's Gospel, Jesus says to Nicodemus, a ruler of the Jews, "Truly, truly I say to you, unless one is born again, anew, one cannot see the kingdom of God" (John 3:3 adapted). I count seven times in the four Gospels Jesus makes the point.

Then, the text says, he took the children in his arms (*in his arms!*), and blessed them and laid his hands on them.

BECOMING LIKE A CHILD

What is this "becoming like a child" that is a prerequisite to our entering the kingdom? Surely it cannot be purity or innocence, or we'd never make it. All that we adults can muster is fleeting purity and false innocence.

But there are some qualities of a child that seem crucial to life in the kingdom: wide-open wonder and wide-open need.

Children have a natural wonder; they notice everything, are open to surprise, are endlessly curious. "The kingdom of God is among you," (Luke 17:21, NRSV), Jesus said; open your eyes and see it. Our children teach us a wide-open wonder and lead us by the hand into the kingdom.

And wide-open need. Children will let you know when they are hungry, when they are hurt, when they feel bad, and when they need to be held. Only later do we stop speaking our need. The kingdom of God belongs to those who know their need. The kingdom of God is the kingdom of the needy— then later, a kingdom *to* the needy.

What is the childlikeness necessary for the kingdom? Let us add vulnerability—the willingness to be vulnerable. It is automatic in children; it takes courage as an adult.

But to be a child in Jesus' day was also to be without status. We come into the kingdom with nothing in our hands, nothing to buy or trade. Think about it: How else can we open our hands to receive the kingdom except as we let go of everything that we carry to bargain our way through life? As the Southern novelist Flannery O'Connor put it, "You accept grace the quickest when you have the least."[4]

RECEIVING CHILDREN, RECEIVING CHRIST

Several times Jesus caught his disciples arguing over who would be the greatest in the kingdom. That's quite comical. If we come into the kingdom without status, how can we clamor for status once inside?

Once when the disciples were arguing the question of greatness, Jesus took a child from the crowd and placed the little one before them and said again, "Unless you become as a child, you will never enter the kingdom of God." In Mark he adds this extraordinary note: "Whoever receives *one such child* in my name receives me; and whoever receives me, receives not me but the one who sent me" (Mark 9:37 emphasis added).

Can we accept the staggering simplicity of this? We meet Christ as we welcome children. The more-than-historical Jesus waits for us in the least of these, including the children. He is saying, "Receive them, receive me. Receive them, receive the One who sent me."

CHILDREN AND THE CRY FOR JUSTICE

One more note, jarring but crucial. Jesus' love was not only tender and affectionate; it also was fierce in its protection of children. So in Matthew, we hear him say, "If any of you put a stumbling block before one of these little ones who believe in me, it would be better for you if a great millstone were fastened around your neck and you were drowned in the depth of the sea" (Matthew 18:6, NRSV).

Here is the prophetic ministry of Jesus coming to the fore again. Many have followed in his steps, including Marion Wright Edelman, the founder of the Children's Defense Fund. The organization published these statistics in 2015. In the United States, more than 15.5 million children are poor, and almost 6.8 million children live in extreme poverty.[5] In North Carolina (my home state):

- 24.3% of children live in poverty, and that percentage is disproportionately higher among children of color.
- More than 1 in 10 children live in extreme poverty.
- More than 26% of children live in households lacking adequate access to food.
- 6.3% of children lack health insurance, while 91.6% participate in Medicaid or the state's CHIP program.
- In FY2012 the annual expenditure per prison inmate was 3.4 times the expenditure per public school child.
- 65% of fourth graders can not read at grade level.[6]

What would Jesus think? We should haul millstones to our state houses and U.S. Congress and put one at the door of every elected official. In Jesus' name.

NOTES

1. For example, Marcia J. Bunge, ed., *The Child in the Bible* (Grand Rapids: Eerdmans, 2008). See also Bunge's essay "Children, the Image of God, and Christology: Theological Anthropology in Solidarity with Children," in *Who Is Jesus Christ for Us Today? Pathways to Contemporary Christology*, ed. Andreas Schuele and Günter Thomas (Louisville: Westminster John Knox Press, 2009), 167–84.

2. Mary Gordon, "The Gospel according to Saint Mark," in *Incarnation: Contemporary Writers on the New Testament*, ed. Alfred Corn (New York: Viking, 1990), 19.

3. Robert Frost, "The Death of the Hired Man," in Robert Frost, *The Poetry of Robert Frost*, ed. Edward Connery Lathem (New York: Holt, Rinehart and Winston, 1969), 38.

4. Flannery O'Connor, *The Habit of Being: Letters*, ed. Sally Fitzgerald (New York: Farrar, Straus & Giroux, 1979), 241.

5. See Children's Defense Fund, "Child Poverty in America 2014: National Analysis," September 16, 2015, http://www.childrensdefense.org/library/poverty-report/child-poverty-in-america-2014.pdf.

6. See Children's Defense Fund, "Children in the States: North Carolina," September 2015," http://www.childrensdefense.org/library/data/state-data-repository/cits/2015/2015-north-carolina-children-in-the-states.pdf.

17

JESUS AND PRAYER

As we believe so we pray. Prayer is an expression of our basic theology. To see how Jesus prayed and what he taught about it is to know Jesus better.[1]

JESUS' RHYTHM OF PRAYER

As an observant first-century Jew, Jesus participated in the regular, three-prayers-a-day rhythm of Jewish piety: morning, afternoon, evening. Morning and afternoon prayer included the *Shema*:

Hear, O Israel:
The Lord is our God;
the Lord is one.

The afternoon prayer featured the *Tephillah*, whose first benediction proclaims:

Blessed art thou, Yahweh,
God of Abraham, God of Isaac, God of Jacob,
the most high God, Master of heaven and earth,
our shield and the shield of our fathers.[2]

The early church adopted this rhythm of prayer by praying the Lord's Prayer three times a day.[3] The early Christians would have been unlikely to carry this rhythm on had not Jesus been faithful in his daily discipline of prayer.

Jesus prayed the Hebrew blessings before and after meals. Before the meal he prayed, "Blessed be thou, Lord our God, king of the world, Who makest bread to come forth from the earth."[4] After the meal was a three-part thanksgiving, the *Birkat Hamazon*, which combined a prayer for mercy upon Israel with a prayer of thanksgiving for nourishment and for the land.[5]

Jesus prayed the prayers of the weekly Shabbat service in the synagogue, "as was his custom" (Luke 4:16), which included the *Shema* and the *Tephillah* and concluded with the *Kaddish*, which formed the background of Jesus' "Lord's Prayer":

> *May his great name be magnified and sanctified*
> *in the world that he created according to his good pleasure!*
> *May he make his reign prevail*
> *during your life and during your days,*
> *and during the life of the entire house of Israel*
> *at this very moment and very soon.*
> *   And let them say: Amen!*[6]

Jesus engaged in extemporaneous and private prayer. To describe his prayer life from within Israel's traditional prayers does not tell us enough. The Gospels portray him as one who spent hours, even whole nights, in solitary prayer:

> And in the morning, a great while before day, he rose and went out to a lonely place, and there he prayed. (Mark 1:35)

> And after he had taken leave of them, he went up on the mountain to pray. (Mark 6:46)

Especially before important decisions, Jesus went aside for concentrated prayer: "In these days he went out to the mountain to pray; and all night he continued in prayer to God. And when it was day, he called his disciples" (Luke 6:12-13).

He also taught his disciples to observe a rhythm of action and prayer: "The apostles returned to Jesus, and told them all that they had done and taught. And he said to them, 'Come away by yourselves to a lonely place, and rest a while'" (Mark 6:30-31).

Jesus prayed prayers of blessing and intercession. As we have seen, he prayed for children and, laying his hands on them, blessed them (Mark 10:16). He also prayed for his friends (John 17), for Jerusalem, and for his nation Israel (Luke 19:41-42).

For Jesus, prayer was at times a spiritual combat with the forces of evil in the world. These were no wimpy prayers, but rather a call to arms: "Watch and pray, lest you enter into temptation" (Matthew 26:41). On one occasion, Jesus' disciples came back discouraged because their spiritual power was insufficient to drive out certain evil spirits. Jesus replied, "This kind cannot be driven out by anything but prayer" (Mark 9:29).

In Luke's Gospel, Jesus described his prayer for Peter in the face of Peter's spiritual testing: "Simon, Simon, behold, Satan demanded to have you, that he might sift you like wheat, but I have prayed for you that your faith may not fail; and when you have turned again, strengthen your brethren" (Luke 22:31-32). There is little doubt that Jesus saw prayer as a way of garnering the power of God in face of the power of evil.

JESUS' TEACHING ON PRAYER

We also learn of Jesus' way of prayer by his teaching about prayer. It was one of the things that spiritual masters taught their disciples. So Jesus' disciples asked, "Lord, teach us to pray" (Luke 11:1). In answer, Jesus taught at least these things:

1. No show-off prayers
2. No long-winded prayers
3. Persistent and unashamed prayers

First, no show-off prayers. In Matthew 6:1, Jesus warned against parading prayer in public:

> Beware of practicing your piety before others in order to be seen by them. . . . And whenever you pray, do not be like the hypocrites; for they love to stand and pray in the synagogues and at the street corners, so that they may be seen by others. (Matthew 6:1,5, NRSV)

Here, Jesus forbids not public prayer—he himself prayed publicly—but rather the kind of prayer we pray *in order to be seen by others*. He called those who do so "hypocrites," which literally means, "play actors."

It is important to remember who it is to whom we pray: God alone. No one else matters. An anecdote is told about Bill Moyers when he was press secretary for President Lyndon B. Johnson. Johnson asked Moyers to pray at some state dinner. Mid-prayer, Johnson interrupted and said, "Speak up, Bill, I can't hear you." Moyers replied, "Mr. President, you are not the one I'm talking to."

Second, Jesus put a taboo on long-winded prayers. They need not go on and on.

> And in praying do not heap up empty phrases as the Gentiles do; for they think they will be heard for their many words. Do not be like them, for your *Abba* knows what you need before you ask him. (Matthew 6:7-8 adapted)

Jesus was forbidding not repetitive prayer in general, but rather the kind of prayer that believes that it can, by its way of praying, earn God's favor or wear God down until God finally listens. It warns against magical praying—*abracadabra*—which believes that certain words will command God's answering our prayers. God's favor, Jesus said, is already with you, God's ear already inclined. No need to go on and on. God is your loving *Abba*, who already knows your need and is on the way to help.

Why, then, pray for long periods of time in solitude, as Jesus did? It is to open oneself to God's presence and guidance, to train one's ear for God's voice, as eyes adjust to the dark.

Third, Jesus urged persistent, unashamed prayer. In one of Jesus' parables (Luke 11:5-8), a man's friend comes to visit, and the man has no food to give to his friend. So he goes to his neighbor's house at midnight to ask for food. The neighbor gives him what he needs—even at midnight—not because of friendship but because of his friend's *anaideia*. Often that word is translated as "persistence," but more accurately, it is describing the petitioner as being "shameless."[7] The man overcame shame to go ask for help.

God welcomes our voice at any time. So go unashamed before God, who loves you as a beloved child.

THE NINE PRAYERS OF JESUS

Jesus prayed nine prayers in the Gospels. The most important was what we call the Lord's Prayer or the Our Father. It could also be called the Model Prayer or the Daily Prayer. Joachim Jeremias wrote, "Jesus appeared in this world with a new prayer."[8] E. F. Scott reminds us that Jesus left his followers not a creed, but a prayer.[9]

THE DAILY PRAYER, OR LORD'S PRAYER

Our Abba in heaven,
hallowed be your name.
Your kingdom come.
Your will be done on earth as in heaven.
Give us today our daily bread.
Forgive us our sins
as we forgive those who sin against us.

Save us in the time of trial
and deliver us from evil.
For yours is the kingdom
and the power and the glory
now and forever.
Amen.
(Matthew 6:9-13 [my translation]; parallel Luke 11:2-4)

The prayer begins, "Our *Abba*." This is the Aramaic word that Jesus spoke, rendered in Greek as *patēr*. This single word conveyed the heart of Jesus' spirituality: the experience of God as perfectly loving Parent. It was an intimate word: Daddy, Papa. It conveyed the trust, intimacy, confidence, and obedience that Jesus felt in his relationship with God. Jesus began eight of his nine prayers with *Abba,* with the exception being his prayer from the cross, which quoted Psalm 22:1: "My God, my God, why have you forsaken me?" (NRSV).

Normally the word *patēr* is translated as "father." I choose to use the Aramaic word that Jesus spoke, *Abba*. Think of a child's first attempt at naming his father, or of an adult's favorite name for her dad.

Most scholarship, notably from that of Jeremias on, recognizes the uniqueness of Jesus' use of *Abba*—not absolutely unique, because contemporary Jews also used the word occasionally, but unique in the consistency and intensity with which Jesus prayed, *Abba*.

The Lord's Prayer begins, "Our *Abba*"; thus, it is a community prayer. We share in Jesus' *Abba* experience. Then, the prayer adds "in heaven." God's *Abba*-ness is beyond that of any earthly parent.

Then come three God-centered and world-oriented petitions:

1. Thy name be hallowed in reverent praise.
2. Thy kingdom come; now in fullness.
3. Thy will be done on earth as in heaven.

These are dangerous, life-altering, world-rearranging prayers.

Then there are three petitions for ourselves as we live our everyday lives:

1. for daily bread;
2. for daily forgiveness and forgivingness;
3. for protection in the face of temptation and evil.

We now turn to the other eight prayers of Jesus. To ponder them is to glimpse who Jesus was.

A PRAYER OF THANKSGIVING AMID LIFE'S REVERSALS

I thank you, Abba,
Lord of heaven and earth,
that you have hidden these things
from the wise and learned
and revealed them to little ones;
yes, Abba, for such was your gracious will.
(Matthew 11:25-26, NRSV [adapted])

Even in the face of opposition, Jesus prayed with thankfulness and trust.

THE GETHSEMANE PRAYER

Abba, Father, all things are possible to you.
Remove this cup from me!
Yet, not what I want, but what you want.
(Mark 14:36 [my translation])

We see the agony of Jesus' petition and his utter yielding to God.

THE PRAYERS FROM THE CROSS

"*Abba*, forgive them; for they know not what they do"
(Luke 23:34 adapted).

"Eli, Eli, lama sabach-thani?" that is, "My God, my God, why hast thou forsaken me?" (Matthew 27:46).

"*Abba*, into thy hands I commit my spirit!" (Luke 23:46 adapted).

Here are three foundational prayers: the prayer of forgiveness, the prayer of abandonment, the prayer of relinquishment.

PRAYERS FROM JOHN'S GOSPEL

Jesus' prayer at Lazarus's tomb before Lazarus is raised from the dead is a supreme expression of Jesus' trust in *Abba*:

> "*Abba*, I thank you that you for having heard me. I knew that you always hear me." (John 11:41-42, NRSV [adapted])

John's Gospel includes a parallel to the Gethsemane prayer. It is Jesus' expression of resolute trust in God:

> *Now is my soul troubled.*
> *And what shall I say,*
> *"Abba, save me from this hour?"*
> *No, for this purpose I have come to this hour.*
> *Abba, glorify your name.*
> (John 12:27-28 adapted)

The key verse of what is known as Jesus' "high priestly prayer" (John 17) communicates the oneness with God that was at the heart of Jesus' prayers:

> *Holy Abba, keep them in your name*
> *which you have given to me,*
> *that they may be one,*
> *even as we are one.*
> (John 17:11b adapted)

To perceive how Jesus prayed is a window into who he was and the character of his faith.

NOTES

1. For a fuller treatment on Jesus and prayer, see H. Stephen Shoemaker, *Finding Jesus in His Prayers* (Nashville: Abingdon Press, 2004).

2. Cited in Joachim Jeremias, *New Testament Theology: The Proclamation of Jesus* (New York: Scribner, 1971), 63.

3. See *Didache* 8:3. The *Didache* was the earliest church manual, dating from late first century to mid-second century.

4. Jeremias, *New Testament Theology*, 185.

5. Cited in Lucien Deiss, ed., *Springtime of the Liturgy: Liturgical Texts of the First Four Centuries*, trans. Matthew J. O'Connell (Collegeville, MN: Liturgical Press, 1979), 5–9.

6. Ibid., 17.

7. Bernard Brandon Scott, *Hear Then a Parable: A Commentary on the Parables of Jesus* (Minneapolis: Fortress Press, 1989), 88.

8. Jeremias, *New Testament Theology*, 186.

9. E. F. Scott, *The Lord's Prayer: Its Character, Purpose, and Interpretation* (New York: Scribner, 1951), 55.

18

JESUS THE FRIEND

In the theological study of Jesus Christ—what we call Christology—Jesus is traditionally described with three names: "prophet," "priest," "king." German theologian Jürgen Moltmann breaks with tradition by offering "friend" as an additional christological title.[1]

The church is the community of Christ. Prophet, priest, and king have a hierarchical bent to them. Is there a language for Jesus and for the community that can escape the language of domination? Yes, it is the language of friendship.

Hymns of the church capture this motif. In 1855 Joseph Scriven marveled in his lyrics, "What a Friend we have in Jesus, / all our sins and griefs to bear!" And in 1910 J. Wilbur Chapman proclaimed:

Jesus! What a Friend for sinners!
Jesus! Lover of my soul;
Friends may fail me, foes assail me,
He, my Savior, makes me whole.

Such songs have become heart-hymns because they express the wonder of Jesus becoming our friend just as we are—"warts and all."

In popular piety, Jesus is often pictured as Friend. Many Christians have experienced Jesus in this way. The question becomes: Does Jesus the Friend fit with the Gospels' portrait of him? Why or why not?

JESUS, FRIEND OF SINNERS

There are two main places in the Gospels where Jesus is called "friend." The first we've already seen: "Look, a glutton and drunkard, a friend of tax collectors and sinners!" (Matthew 11:19, NRSV). The word *friend* was meant as a sneer. Jesus took it as a badge of honor.

In a world as afraid of the contagiousness of sin as a hypochondriac is afraid of germs, Jesus set forth a contagion of holiness, the kingdom of God, a contagion of the goodness of God. "As a friend," Moltmann comments, "Jesus offers the unlovable the friendship of God."[2]

When we feel most unlovable, we experience the friendship of Jesus. But Jesus loves the lovable part of us too, what is lovable in us all. When he ate with tax collectors and sinners, he did not hold his nose. He was not "slumming" from heaven for a little while to make a theological point. He *liked* these people, ate and drank with them, enjoyed them. Can we believe this? Maybe he likes us too, and enjoys us.

A sinner known as Matthew the tax collector became part of Jesus' inner circle of disciples. The Twelve were not just symbols (that is, symbols of the renewed twelve tribes of Israel); they were friends too. Who wants to be someone's symbol? This bringing of the divine friendship was transformative, as the transformation of Zacchaeus the tax collector showed.

Theologically, God is often described in two dimensions: "transcendent" and "imminent," or the "otherness" of God and the "alongsideness" of God. Jesus spoke to his disciples about the Holy Spirit, known in John's Gospel as the Paraclete, who would come to them after he died, come to them as he had come to them. "Paraclete" means "to be called alongside." Jesus was and is the alongsideness of God, the alongsideness to us all.

FRIENDSHIP IN JOHN'S GOSPEL

The other place where "Jesus" and "friend" are spoken of in the same breath is in John's Gospel. The context is Jesus' final teaching to his disciples placed between the Last Supper and his arrest. It is his last will and testament, his blessing on them before he died:

> This is my commandment, that you love one another as I have loved you. No one has greater love than this, to lay down one's life for one's friends. You are my friends if [as] you do what I command you. I do not call you servants any longer, because the servant does not know what the master is doing; but I have called you friends, because I have made known to you everything that I have heard from my *Abba*. (John 15:12-15, NRSV [adapted])

Note here the movement from servant to friend. Jesus has held nothing back. If knowledge is power, he has shared power. Everything that God revealed to Jesus, Jesus revealed to his disciples, and he reveals to us.

Note too that friendship with Jesus involves following his commands, the most important of which was "Love one another as I have loved you." Friendship means taking up common cause.

Note also that the supreme act of friendship is to give one's life for a friend. Friends are willing to sacrifice for the well-being of a friend. Jesus, the supreme Friend, would do so on the cross. As John put it: loving us, he loved us to the end (see John 13:1).

"Friend" is not only a christological title for Jesus; it is also a name for the church as a community of friends. The

Quakers, begun in England in the second half of the seventeenth century, have caught this spirit as they call themselves the Religious Society of Friends. A nonhierarchical community of faith, the Quakers minimize the distinction between "clergy" and "laity." They affirm that God has called them all as equals in the church.

The main distinctive doctrine of Quakers is that of the "Inner Light," which they believe everyone has. Jesus is speaking to us all, befriending us. This doctrine gives dignity to all persons, in and out of the church. The Quakers were among the first in America to give up slaves if they owned them and to work for the abolition of slavery. The renowned Quaker leader John Woolman wore only white suits because they had no dye, which came from a slave-based industry. Quakers have majored in service to those in need and education. Friends of Jesus indeed!

What do friends do? They love. They love as equals. The Greek word for "friend" (*philos* and *philē*) has its root in the verb for "love," *phileo*. (As Philadelphia is the city of brotherly/sisterly [-*adelphia*] love [*phil-*]). New Testament scholar Gail O'Day translates this Greek word for "friends" as "those who are loved."[3]

OTHER EXAMPLES OF FRIENDSHIP

One of Jesus' dearest groups of friends was Martha, Mary, and Lazarus—his Bethany family. Jesus spent the night with them as he traveled through Bethany to Jerusalem, only a couple of miles away. Theirs was the home where the Son of Man, who had no place to lay his head, could find rest. Luke 10:38-42 tells the memorable story in which Martha welcomed Jesus into her home and began to cook for him while Mary sat at his feet listening to him teach. Martha grew irritated that Mary was not helping her in the kitchen and said to Jesus, "Lord, do you not care that my sister has left me to serve alone? Tell her then to help me" (Luke 10:40). Jesus replied, "Martha, Martha, you are anxious and troubled about many things; one thing is needful. Mary has chosen the good portion, which shall not be taken away from her" (Luke 10:41-42). We see Martha serving as a friend, Mary learning as a friend, and Jesus confronting Martha as a friend.

When Lazarus grew ill, Mary and Martha sent messengers to Jesus to say, "He whom you love is ill" (John 11:3). When Jesus was en route to Bethany, Martha met him and said with grief's anger, "Lord, if you had been here my brother would not have died"; Jesus replied, "Your brother will rise again" (John 11:21,23).

When Martha agreed that, yes, Lazarus would rise in the resurrection of the last day, then Jesus declared, "I am the resurrection and the life" (John 11:25). Martha responded with a supreme confession of faith, equal to Peter's: "I believe that you are the Christ, the Son of God, he who is coming into the world" (John 11:27). Martha has listened to Jesus teach too! Friends are free to express their rawest emotions to one another.

When Jesus arrived in Bethany and saw that Lazarus had died, the Scripture says, "Jesus wept" (John 11:35). Onlookers said, "See how much Jesus loved him!" (John 11:36 [my translation]). Who can miss the tenderness of Jesus' relation with his Bethany family?

We watch friendship in action in his deep friendship with Mary Magdalene, an intimate friendship, perhaps unique among his disciples. He had freed her of seven demons, and she had become part of the group of disciples who followed Jesus and supported him out of their resources (see Luke 8:1-3). It was she who was at the crucifixion, the burial, and empty tomb. It was she to whom the Risen Jesus appeared first in John's Gospel. "Mary," he called her, and she answered back, "Rabbouni," or "my dear rabbi." *The Gospel of Mary* (Magdalene), discovered in 1896, pictures the remarkable, unique role that Mary played among the disciples and her singular closeness to Jesus.

THE RECEIVING OF FRIENDSHIP

Jesus gave friendship in his relationship with people. Did he receive friendship? Clearly in his relationship with Mary, Martha, and Lazarus, he received from them. As they needed him, he needed them.

His disciples were friends. Perhaps Jesus was closest to three, Peter, James and John. When he went up the mountain for his transfiguration, he took Peter, James and John with him. When he healed the twelve year-old girl, he took only these three into the girl's house where he healed her (Mark 5:37).

On the night of his last supper, betrayal, and arrest, he went to pray in the garden of Gethsemane (Mark 14:32-42). He asked Peter, James, and John to pray with him. "Abba, Father, all things are possible to thee; remove this cup from me, yet not what I will, but what thou wilt" (Mark 14:36). In agonized petition he prayed to be released from his coming death; and in deep yielding he offered his life into God's hands. In his darkest moment needed these three with him. But what did they do? They fell asleep. Three times Jesus caught them asleep and asked them to watch and pray with him lest they "enter into temptation" (Mark 14:38). The night was a night of spiritual testing for them all. Jesus needed them. They needed to be praying but fell asleep.

In friendship we give and receive. So did Jesus in his true humanity.

Some picture God as "all-sufficient" with no need of us, but the Bible paints a different picture. In Isaiah, God called Abraham "my friend" (Isaiah 41:8). In Exodus 33:11 we read, "Thus the LORD used to speak to Moses face-to-face as one speaks to a friend" (NRSV). God needs friends to carry out the divine mission in the world.

And Jesus needed friends for companionship and joy and comradeship in the common cause of the kingdom.

Can we let Jesus come that close to us? To use Henri Nouwen's image, the friendship of Jesus moves us from a "house of fear" to a "house of love." As Jesus' friends, we experience the divine friendship and dwell in love.

NOTES

1. See Jürgen Moltmann, *The Church in the Power of the Spirit: A Contribution to Messianic Eschatology*, trans. Margaret Kohl (New York: Harper & Row, 1977), 114–21; idem, *A Broad Place: An Autobiography*, trans. Margaret Kohl (Minneapolis: Fortress Press, 2008), 202–11.

2. Moltmann, *The Church in the Power of the Spirit*, 117.

3. Gail O'Day, "John," in *The New Interpreter's Bible*, ed. Leander E. Keck (Nashville: Abingdon Press, 1995), 9:758.

19

JESUS THE STRANGER

"Yes'm," the Misfit said as if he agreed. "Jesus thrown everything off balance."

—Flannery O'Connor[1]

Jesus came not only as friend, but also as stranger. The one we thought we knew, we do not. He now appears as strange, other, even enemy. Why else was he crucified? Blasphemer, heretic, seditionist, disturber of the fragile Roman peace—he must go. New Testament scholar Leander Keck writes, "Only the Jesus who is other, different, intriguing, frustraing, fascinating can change what one really is. A Jesus who is like the self only reinforces what is already in the self. And changing the self is precisely what his role in the moral life is all about."[2]

It may seem odd to describe Jesus as stranger, but this may be the only way to make sure we have seen him as he is, not as what we want him to be. "He comes to us as one unknown," Albert Schweitzer said to those too smug about who Jesus was and is (see the Preface).

Author and theologian Frederick Buechner describes a Maundy Thursday sermon that he heard in an Episcopal church in Wheaton, Illinois. The preacher was preaching on

Peter's denial on the night of Jesus' arrest. "I do not know the man!" Peter exclaimed to those who questioned him about his association with Jesus. These words, said the preacher, were not only a lie; they were also the truth. They were not only a denial; they were also a confession. After three years of following Jesus, listening, watching, Peter still did not know the man.

Perhaps this is where we begin with Jesus the stranger. Unless we know that we do not know him, we cannot grow to know him. In Christian spirituality and theology, there are what scholars call the *via positiva* and the *via negativa*.

The *via positiva* is also called *kataphatic* theology. It is about the God we can know. It uses words, concepts, images. In contrast, the *via negativa* is called *apophatic* theology. It recognizes that we do not know, or cannot know. It is the path of unknowing. On this path we go wordless; we put aside images, thoughts, concepts, and theologies in order to find a deeper knowing. We are willing to enter into what the Romantic poet John Keats called "negative capability," where we become "capable of being in uncertainties, Mysteries, doubts without any irritable reaching after fact & reason."[3]

What we thought we knew, we do not. Who we thought he was, he is not. The medieval theologian Anselm said there is a "higher ignorance" that is "faith seeking understanding." As abolitionist and women's rights activist Sojourner Truth said of her encounter with the living Jesus, "I know you and don't know you."

JESUS' FIRST SERMON AT NAZARETH

In Luke 4:16-30 we observe how quickly Jesus changed from friend to stranger to enemy in his hometown. Soon after his baptism, he went to the synagogue in Nazareth for a Shabbat service and preached his "inaugural sermon" for his old neighbors. He was invited to read from the Prophets and read from Isaiah 61:

The Spirit of the Lord is upon me,
because God has anointed me
to bring good news to the poor.
God has sent me
to proclaim release to the captives
and recovery of sight to the blind,
to let the oppressed go free,
to proclaim the year of the Lord's favor.
(Luke 4:18-19, NRSV [adapted])

He rolled up the scroll, and then he sat, in good rabbinic fashion, to teach. "Today this scripture is fulfilled," he said. *Today.*

The congregation nodded an approval. He was Judy Garland singing "Happy Days Are Here Again." God's messianic kingdom was dawning! Perhaps one listener punched his friend and, with a hint of local pride, said, "That's Joe's boy, isn't it?"

Then Jesus began to interpret the text, and as he did, the mood shifted sharply. The kingdom was here all right, but not as they expected. It was coming to foreigners, to outsiders. Jesus gave examples. There were many widows in Israel in Elijah's time during the great drought, but Elijah was sent (meaning, by God!) to a widow in Sidon. There were many lepers in Elijah's day, but he cured a leper named Naaman, a Syrian general.

The kingdom's here, but in Havana not Nashville. Healing's happening, but look! It's a Shiite general in Basra who has been healed. God's salvation is beyond our clan, our nation, even our brand of faith. The kingdom of God is not the kingdom of Israel, he was saying. It is larger.

All of a sudden, Jesus the homeboy became Jesus the stranger. The congregation was filled with rage, Luke tells us, and they seized him, carried him to a cliff and tried to throw him off. That's not how you picture the response to your first sermon.

JESUS THE STRANGER, NOW AND THEN

But this was not the only time Jesus was seen as stranger, other, different, enemy. At one point, the Gospels report that Jesus' family came to take him forcibly home because people were saying that he was "out of his mind" (in Greek, *exestē*) (Mark 3:21).

In Elie Wiesel's Holocaust memoir, *Night*, he tells of a member of his village when he was growing up. They called him "Moishe the Beadle." He was awkward and shy, but he was one possessed by God and every day chanted his song to God. He became Elie Wiesel's teacher in Kabbalah, the tradition of Jewish mysticism.

Then one day all the "foreign Jews" were expelled from his village, and Moishe was taken away by train. Days, weeks, months passed; then suddenly Moishe was back.

He told Wiesel what happened. The train had crossed the border; then the Gestapo took over. The Jews were paraded into the forest. They were forced to dig huge trenches. Then they were lined up, shot, and pushed into the massive graves. Children were tossed into the air and used as targets for machine guns. Tobie the tailor begged to die before his sons were killed. Moishe somehow escaped. He had been shot in the leg and left for dead.

Then he began to go from one Jewish home to another, telling them what had happened. No one believed him. They thought he was imagining things. Some thought that he had gone mad. Even Wiesel, his student, did not believe him. Such horror could not happen.[4]

Sometimes our "see-ers" and prophets are thought to be mad. Insane. Out of their minds.

In response to Jesus' acts of healing and deliverance, some accused him of being demon-possessed, in league with Beelzebub the prince of demons. In John's Gospel some adversaries came and said, "Are we not right in saying that you are a Samaritan and have a demon?" (John 8:48, NRSV).

Jesus answered with deliberate evasiveness: "I don't have a demon." Jesus would not let the charge of demon possession stand. His power came from God, not Satan. But he did not answer the Samaritan question. He let it linger in the air. It's an interesting accusation and a shocking association: Jesus the Samaritan, the outsider, despised and rejected, mixed race, heterodox, other.

Jesus told a surprising parable with a Samaritan as the hero. He brought the kingdom of God to a Samaritan woman, an outsider herself, and then enlisted her in his mission. He healed a group of ten lepers, one a Samaritan, and the nine others Jews, and only the Samaritan came back to thank him and praise God. Then, by God, Jesus must be a closet Samaritan!

Jesus was willing to be an outsider so that we might recognize that there is no outsider to God. Jesus says: I am a Cuban, an Indian, a South African, a Jew; I am a Sunni, a Buddhist, Sufi, Sikh; I am black, gay, womanish, and Latino/Latina.[5] I am *human*, created in the image of God, come as a stranger so there will be no more strangers in the household of God and God's earth.

Are we willing to let Jesus come to us as a stranger, as unknown? Jesus the friend represents the radical immanence of God, the nearness of God beyond imagining. Jesus as stranger represents the radical transcendence of God, the otherness, the difference of God beyond imagining. As God said through the prophet Isaiah,

> *For my thoughts are not your thoughts,*
> *neither are your ways my ways, says the* LORD.
> *For as the heavens are higher than the earth,*
> *so are my ways higher than your ways*
> *and my thoughts than your thoughts.*
> (Isaiah 55:8-9)

Theologian Dietrich Bonhoeffer, in his classic book *Life Together*, spoke of the word of God that comes to us from outside us—*extra nos*. The word of God that comes to us in the voice of *another*.[6] To be sure, God's word is also near us, within us, "in your mouth and in your heart" (Deuteronomy 30:14). But sometimes the word of God must come from *another* place, foreign and strange, upsetting our conventional thinking, our settled truths, our assumed beliefs.

The Welsh poet Waldo Williams gives us numerous images of Jesus the outsider, the stranger, the riddler of the kingdom that comes to shatter and rearrange all our kingdoms. Here are some of his images: the outlaw, the huntsman, the lost heir, the exiled king, the one who escapes the conscription of every army.[7]

Will we let Jesus the stranger through? Welcome him? Will we let him bring the kingdom he would bring rather than the one we have devised? Author and mystic Richard Rohr told our congregation at Myers Park Baptist Church that when we pray, "Thy kingdom come," we are praying, "My kingdom go."

Jesus was willing to become a stranger that we might open our eyes to the kingdom of God, which was coming to rearrange things in this world. And so were his followers willing to be strange, different, other, in order to witness the life of Christ in them. The apostle Paul wrote, "For I think God has exhibited the apostles as last of all. . . . We have become a spectacle to the world. . . . We are fools for Christ's sake" (1 Corinthians 4:9-10).

To acknowledge Jesus the stranger is to recognize that there is a dimension of Jesus that will always be, in the language of the poet Gerard Manley Hopkins, "counter, original, spare, strange."[8] It is to enter into a reverent knowing and unknowing. The quest for the historical Jesus will never be finished. Our certainties about him are always ready to be upset. One day he is Friend; another day he is stranger.

This reverent knowing and unknowing keeps our faith alive as we seek to know and follow Jesus. Author and poet Maya Angelou said that when overly zealous, overly certain people came to her and announced, "I am a Christian," she answered, "Already?"[9]

We must allow Jesus to be a stranger lest our discipleship be chasing our own tails.

NOTES

1. Flannery O'Connor, "A Good Man Is Hard to Find," in Flannery O'Connor, *Collected Works* (New York: Library of America, 1988), 151.

2. Leander E. Keck, *Who Is Jesus? History in the Perfect Tense* (Columbia, SC: University of South Carolina Press, 2000), 162.

3. John Keats, *Selected Poems and Letters of John Keats*, ed. Douglas Bush (Boston: Houghton Mifflin; Riverside Press, 1959), 261.

4. Eli Wiesel, *Night*, trans. Stella Rodway (New York: Hill and Wang, 1954), 22–23.

5. For an example of "Jesus as stranger" theology, see Jesus as the Black Jesus and Black Christ in the work of James H. Cone: *God of the Oppressed* (New York: Seabury Press, 1975); idem, *A Black Theology of Liberation* (Philadelphia: Lippincott, 1970).

6. Dietrich Bonhoeffer, *Life Together*, trans. John W. Doberstein (New York: Harper & Row, 1954), 22–23.

7. Waldo Williams, "Between Two Fields," in Rowan Williams, *The Poems of Rowan Williams* (Oxford: Perpetua Press, 2002), 92–93. Rowan Williams translated "Between Two Fields" from the Welsh. There is a variant translation that Roman Williams made of one line, "the one who escapes the conscription of every army" from his *Open to Judgement: Sermons and Addresses* (London: Darton, Longman & Todd, 1984), 131.

8. Gerard Manley Hopkins, "Pied Beauty," in Gerard Manley Hopkins, *The Poems of Gerard Manley Hopkins*, ed. W. H. Gardner and N. H. MacKenzie (New York: Oxford University Press, 1970), 70.

9. Maya Angelou, in a 2011 White House interview. www.telegraph.co.uk /culture/culturevideo/10861920/Maya-Angelou-Im-trying-to-be-a-Chrisitian.html (accessed August 1, 2016).

20

JESUS AND FORGIVENESS

Forgiveness is ever the issue: the forgiveness we need to receive and the forgiveness we need to give. The New Testament word for "forgive" means literally "to loose," to set free. It is a kind of deliverance and a kind of healing. Jesus healed and delivered as he offered God's forgiveness. It was forgiveness as both pardon and power.

FORGIVENESS AT THE HEART
OF THE GOSPELS

Forgiveness was at the heart of the gospel that Jesus proclaimed and embodied. He lived with forgiveness ever on his lips. He died with forgiveness on his lips: "Father, forgive them; for they know not what they do" (Luke 23:34). He dared to pronounce God's forgiveness and to say that his own words were God's power to forgive. He left us not with a creed but a prayer, and at the center of the prayer is this petition: "Forgive us our debts—our trespasses, our sins—as we forgive our debtors—those who have trespassed, sinned against us."

In John 20:19-23 we read that on Easter evening, Jesus appeared in his resurrection body to his frightened disciples.

"Peace to you," he said—God's *shalom* coming to forgive those who had deserted him. Then he said it a second time because the human heart can never hear it enough: "Peace to you." Then he said, "As the Father has sent me, so send I you." And then he blew on them his breath and said, "Receive the Holy Spirit," for we cannot do God's work without God's Spirit. And what did Jesus send them out to do? "Go and loose people from their sins," he said.

Forgiveness is central to the kingdom of God, which Jesus announced and brought near in his life. In the Lord's Prayer he linked our two great daily needs: bread and forgiveness. Every day we need bread, and every day we need forgiveness. One nourishes the body; the other sustains the spirit.

One biblical scholar notes that the prayer for forgiveness is the structural center of the Lord's Prayer.[1] Another observes that this prayer is the only petition that explicitly links God's gift to us with our action toward others: "as we too forgive."[2]

There is spiritual and psychological truth here. Picture it this way: We receive God's forgiveness through a double-hinged, swinging door of the heart. If we fasten the door after receiving God's forgiveness and do not let it flow on to others, then we shut the flow of God's everyday forgiveness of us. This prayer helps keep the flow going.

FORGIVENESS IN THE GOSPELS

In the second chapter of Mark's Gospel, we see the drama of forgiveness and healing acted out. Jesus healed a paralyzed man but first pronounced God's forgiveness on him: "Son, your sins are forgiven." The man may have thought, *That's fine, but that's not why I'm here. My legs, Lord.*

Jesus' opponents immediately charged him with blasphemy: "Who can forgive sins but God alone?" (Mark 2:7).

New Testament scholar Andreas Schuele comments that in Hebrew Scriptures there are only two verbs with God as the sole actor: *bara*, "to create," and *salah*, "to forgive."[3] So the accusation of blasphemy was no idle charge. But there may have been a tiny bit of institutional self-interest involved. A religious institution likes to be in control of God's grace, set the conditions for forgiveness, decide who is worthy to take Communion or get into heaven. But here Jesus is pronouncing divine forgiveness, giving it away as free as the air, the sun, the water. This man is a danger to the institution.

So, to prove his power to forgive, Jesus also healed the paralytic! And the man got right up, picked up the mat on which he was carried, and danced a jig—or as much as he could jig after having been paralyzed so long.

Charles Wesley's hymn "O for a Thousand Tongues to Sing" proclaims, "He breaks the power of canceled sin / He sets the prisoner free." Did you catch the phrase "canceled sin"? Sin *already forgiven* can still paralyze us if we do not let the forgiveness in. We may even fight our healing, believing that we don't deserve it because of our sins. Jesus is loosing forgiveness all over, and he does so without the requirement of religious ritual.

FORGIVENESS AND US

The audacity of Jesus' mission was that he was an instrument of what God alone can do: *salah*, forgive. And with double audacity he called his disciples to go do the same.

It is hard to forgive when we ourselves have been harmed by another. Simon Peter, the ever-flawed and ever-eager follower of Jesus, asked him, "Lord, how often shall my brother or sister sin against me, and I forgive? As many as seven times?" (The prevailing teaching of the day said three times.) But Jesus replied, "I do not say to you seven times, but seventy times seven" (Matthew 18:21-22 adapted).

The Greek text of Jesus' reply can also be translated as "seventy-seven times." Do not literalize the numeric value. The point is that we never stop trying to forgive. It may take seventy-seven or 490 times to complete the process.

Sometimes we pray, "Lord, help me forgive." Other times we say, "Lord, help me *want* to forgive." Other times, "Lord, help me *want to want to* forgive." C. S. Lewis wrote in a journal, "Last week, while at prayer, I suddenly discovered—or felt as if I did—that I had really forgiven someone I had been trying to forgive for over thirty years. Trying, and praying that I might."[4]

What Jesus brought was the great flowing forgiveness of the kingdom of God. As those who have received, how can we not pass God's forgiveness on? Jesus told a parable to make the point. The kingdom of heaven is like a king, he said, who was going over his financial books and discovered that a servant entrusted with a massive part of his estate was in arrears by the astronomical sum of ten thousand talents. Here was a mess-up of biblical (or Wall Street) proportions!

The man could never pay back this immense debt. It could not be repaid. The king, in a gesture of breathtaking mercy, forgave the debt.

But what happened? This same man was met by a fellow servant who owed him one hundred denarii, a pittance compared to the debt that had just been forgiven by the king. The other man begged for mercy, for time to repay the money. But the king's servant said no and had him thrown into prison (Matthew 18:23-35). "How could he?" we ask—and then we recognize ourselves as that first man. The parable is about the immensity of God's mercy and how in the kingdom of God we are all *forgiven forgivers*.

Desmond Tutu, archbishop emeritus of Cape Town, says that in his native tongue, Xhosa, one asks for forgiveness with the words *Ndicel' uxolo*: "I ask for peace."[5] And isn't that what the Risen Jesus brought us?

The astonishing news is that before we even ask, God comes in Jesus to say, "Peace be with you." And we get to be part of a peace-giving community, receivers and instruments of God's power to forgive. The stone in the heart is dissolved, and now we sing, "Peace."

NOTES

1. Ulrich Luz, *Matthew 1–7: A Commentary*, trans. James E. Crouch, ed. Helmut Koester (Minneapolis: Fortress Press, 2007), 173.

2. Andreas Schuele, "'On Earth as It Is in Heaven': Eschatology and the Ethics of Forgiveness," in *Who Is Jesus Christ for Us Today? Pathways to Contemporary Christology*, ed. Andreas Schuele and Günter Thomas (Louisville: Westminster John Knox Press, 2009), 185–202.

3. Ibid., 188.

4. C. S. Lewis, *Letters to Malcolm: Chiefly on Prayer* (New York: Harcourt, Brace & World, 1964), 106.

5. Desmond Tutu, "An Invitation to Forgive," December 5, 2014, http://www.huffingtonpost.com/desmond-tutu/an-invitation-to-forgive_b_5050747.html.

PART IV

THE LAST AND FIRST DAYS

21

THE TURN
TOWARD JERUSALEM
AND THE CROSS

Most of Jesus' ministry was set in Galilee. John's Gospel alone describes three trips to Jerusalem. These "Galilean days" were marked by miracles, teaching, and many people following him. At some point in Jesus' ministry, he decided to make his last and decisive journey to Jerusalem, turning his face toward death on a Roman cross. Luke described the transition with these words: "When the days drew near for him to be received up, he set his face to go to Jerusalem" (Luke 9:51).

THE PREDICTIONS OF HIS DEATH

Three times Jesus told his disciples predictions of his coming death,[1] announcements that brought horror, bewilderment, and denial. "No," said Simon Peter, "this must not happen to you."

The most original (earliest and most historic) words of his predictions go like this: "The Son of Man is to be betrayed into human hands, and they will kill him, and three days after being killed, he will rise again" (Mark 9:31, NRSV). Other Gospels fill in the detail that the "men" who handed him over were "elders, chief priests, and scribes." And the later Gospel writers changed "after three days," which means after a short period of time, to "on the third day" to conform to the actual day of Jesus' resurrection.

Jesus knew that the religious leaders were set against him. He had been warned about Herod and had carefully avoided "that fox" in Galilee, but he knew he would not avoid conflict with the Roman authorities in Jerusalem. So Jesus knew that by going up to Jerusalem, he was headed inexorably toward his death.

What was Jesus' hope for resurrection? Most probably it was the hope shared by Pharisees (but not Sadducees) of his time: a general resurrection of all the dead to be followed by the great judgment, after which the righteous would enjoy life with God in the world to come. When Jesus said "three days," he meant *soon*! And most probably what he hoped in was the start of the general resurrection of the dead.

That the Jesus Story would take a different direction is due to the unexpected action of God on Sunday, the third day, when Jesus alone was raised from the dead.[2]

Jesus' conflict with religious leaders was sparked by his presumption in acting on behalf of God and his challenge to the priority of certain ritual practices. He broke the law by healing on the Sabbath. He also healed on the spot, free of the requirement of certain ritual requirements.[3] He criticized religious leaders for their hyperobservance of the letter of the law but ignoring God's greater demand for justice and mercy.

Jesus' conflict with Rome arose from his challenge to the social, economic, and political status quo, a status quo that was oppressive injustice to many. His "good news to the poor" was bad news to the rich—unless they turned and entered the kingdom.

Moreover, his healings and teachings had drawn a large following that posed a threat to the religious and political elite. That he preached nonviolence did not lessen their sense of his danger to them.

JESUS' VIEW OF HIS DEATH

How did Jesus see his approaching death? There was the tradition of the "righteous martyr" dating from the Maccabean revolt, where a martyr's death was seen as bringing the nation's suffering to an end. Such a righteous death would be rewarded by God in the world to come.

There was also the biblical vision of the Suffering Servant in Isaiah:

> *Surely he has borne our griefs and carried our sorrows;*
> *yet we esteemed him stricken, smitten by God, and afflicted.*
> *But he was wounded for our transgressions,*
> *he was bruised for our iniquities;*
> *upon him was the chastisement that makes us whole,*
> *and with his stripes we are healed.*
> (Isaiah 53:4-5)

And there were Jesus' own words: "For the Son of man also came not to be served but to serve, and to give his life as a ransom for many" (Mark 10:45, NRSV). "Ransom" was a word that meant freedom and liberation. In other words, death was his destiny, and his death would be the healing and redemption of the world.

To flee from death would have been a betrayal of Jesus' mission and the integrity of his life. He would die, trusting his life and death into the hands of God.

THE CROSS

When Jesus announced his intention to go to Jerusalem and die, Peter said, "God forbid, Lord! This shall never happen to you" (Matthew 16:22). Just as quickly, Jesus said, "Get behind me, Satan! You are a stumbling block to me; for you are setting your mind not on divine things but on human things" (Matthew 16:23, NRSV).

It is almost impossible to understand how greatly Jesus' revelation of himself as suffering Messiah reversed all the disciples' ways of thinking, feeling, hoping. The Messiah must never suffer. When the Messiah comes, all will be right and all will be well. These were the centuries-old faith convictions of their people. But here, but now, the Messiah had come, and all was not right and all was not well, not yet. Jesus was saying to them that he had come to enter our suffering and to suffer himself.

Then Jesus, looking at his disciples, told them this applied to them as well. If they follow the Messiah, they will suffer too. "If any want to become my followers, let them deny themselves and take up their cross and follow me. For those who want to save their life will lose it, and those who lose their life for my sake, and for the sake of the gospel, will save it" (Mark 8:34-35, NRSV).

We who wear the cross as jewelry today cannot fathom the first-century horror that it represented. This form of execution was reserved for the worst offenders: revolutionaries against the state, violent criminals, and low-class thieves. Roman citizens could be crucified only for high treason. Otherwise the cross was reserved for slaves and foreigners. The body was strung up on a cross of wood.[4] It took a torturously long time for the person to die, and then the corpses were thrown on the trash pile to rot. No more hideous fate could be imagined.

No wonder the apostle Paul called the cross "a stumbling block to Jews and folly to Gentiles" (1 Corinthians 1:23). Justin Martyr, defender of the faith in the next generation, said, "They say that our *madness* consists in the fact that we put a *crucified man* in second place after the unchangeable and eternal God, the Creator of the world."[5]

The Roman statesman Pliny wrote about the "perverse and extravagant superstition" of Christians, that a man honored as God would be nailed to a cross as a common enemy of the state.[6]

Some early graffiti discovered on a Roman palace wall near the Circus Maximus, dated 200 BCE, show a man hanging on a cross, except that instead of a man's head there is the head of a jackass, and scribbled underneath in large letters are these words: ALEXAMENOS WORSHIPS GOD.

In this light it is not hard to understand the dread that Jesus felt as he faced the decision to die in this way, nor to understand the incredulity and horror his disciples felt to think of this fate as their Master's end.

No wonder Peter said, "God forbid, Lord!" And no wonder their horror to hear that they themselves could suffer the cross. Some of his followers would indeed be crucified in the years ahead, but "taking up one's cross" would have broader and less literal meanings.

THE VOCATION OF THE CROSS

Taking up the cross would come to mean taking up the sufferings of others as a cause. It would mean, to quote author and theologian Parker Palmer, being "celebrants, advocates, defenders of the life wherever we find it."[7]

For the Christian theologian Dietrich Bonhoeffer, it meant risking his life for Jews and for his fellow Germans in the face of Adolf Hitler. On April 5, 1943, he was arrested. Exactly two years later, on April 5, 1945, Hitler personally signed the execution order. Bonhoeffer was hanged April 9, 1945. He was thirty-nine years old. His last words were "This is the end—for me the beginning of life."

Bonhoeffer's cross-bearing began in the early 1930s when he began opposing Hitler's policies and warning people about the dangers of the Führer. Twice he came to America to study at Union Theological Seminary. His friends begged him not to return to Germany.

Then came a terrible night known as Kristallnacht, the "Night of Broken Glass," November 9, 1938. This was the night when the violence against the Jews turned openly public. Synagogues, homes, and Jewish places of business were ransacked. Holy books were burned. Broken glass was everywhere—a signal of what the Third Reich intended to do with the Jews.

That night Bonhoeffer opened his Bible, and he began to read Psalm 74:

O God, why do you cast us off forever? . . .
Remember your congregation, which you acquired long ago. . . .
Your foes have roared within your holy place;
    they set up their emblems there.
At the upper entrance they hacked
the wooden trellis with axes. . . .
They set your sanctuary on fire;
    they desecrated the dwelling place of your name,
    bringing it to the ground.
They said to themselves, "We will utterly subdue them";
    they burned all the meeting places of God in the land.
We do not see our emblems;
    there is no longer any prophet,
    and there is no one among us who knows how long.
How long, O God, is the foe to scoff?
(Psalm 74:1-10, NRSV)

Bonhoeffer read that psalm that terrible night and, in the margin of his Bible, wrote his own completion of the question "How long?" He wrote, "How long, O God, shall I be a bystander?"

Perhaps this is at the heart of the calling of the cross: it will not let us be bystanders.

I think of Martin Luther King Jr., heading into the simmering violence of American white supremacy, willing to give his life if necessary. His sermon in Memphis the night before his death was full of foreboding about what was to come but even fuller with hope about God's victory to come no matter what happened.

I think of the famous speech by Nelson Mandela, who said at his trial in Pretoria that harmony and equality are ideals for which he hoped to live and see realized, but if need be, for which he was prepared to die.

The integrity of Jesus' life would not let him flee the prospect of his death. He would see his life as the son/servant of God through to the end, whatever that end might be.

NOTES

1. See Matthew 16:21; 17:22-23; 20:18-19; parallels are in Mark 8:31; 9:31; 10:33-34; Luke 9:22; 9:43-44; 18:31-33.

2. Matthew 27:52-53 says that after Jesus died on the cross, an unspecified number of bodies of the righteous were raised, and after his resurrection they left their tombs and went into Jerusalem and appeared to others. This passage greatly vexes scholars, and many see it as an insertion made after Matthew was written. The fact that this odd event is not mentioned in any of the other Gospels or elsewhere in the New Testament makes it unlikely to have happened.

3. Those healed by Jesus did not have to go to the priests as part of the healing process. Luke alludes to this requirement in Jesus' healing of the ten lepers whom he commanded to go show themselves to the priests (Luke 17:14).

4. For archeological research and drawings of crucifixion, see *Israel Exploration Journal* 20 (1970): 29.

5. Justin Martyr, *First Apology* 13.4, cited in Martin Hengel, *Crucifixion in the Ancient World and the Folly of the Message of the Cross*, trans. John Bowden (Philadelphia: Fortress Press, 1977), 1.

6. Pliny, *Epistles* 10.96.4-8, cited in Hengel, *Crucifixion*, 2.

7. Parker Palmer, *The Active Life: A Spirituality of Work, Creativity, and Caring* (San Francisco: Jossey-Bass, 1999), 8.

22

THE LAST WEEK OF THE HISTORICAL JESUS

The final week of Jesus' life began on the day that Christians call Palm Sunday. Jesus was living true to his mission as the son/servant of God and to the reign of God he had come to proclaim. We will see in this chapter several prophetic action signs, most prominently the "triumphal entry" and the "cleansing of the temple," as well as an accompanying prophecy of the destruction of the temple, a prophetic anointing, and several key confrontations in Jerusalem.

THE ENTRY INTO JERUSALEM

Jesus approached Jerusalem from the Mount of Olives, then down into the valley, and up to the eastern gate into Jerusalem. In Jewish messianic expectation, this was the entrance route of the coming Messiah as he entered God's holy city. Jesus had carefully prepared his entry as a fulfillment of the prophet Zechariah.

But his was not the only procession into the city that week, and the two processions portrayed a clash of kingdoms. Scholars of the historical Jesus describe these two processions that week of Passover.[1]

First was a procession of Pilate, the Roman governor, from the west, traveling from the imperial capital of Caesarea Maritima. He came in the full "panoply of imperial power": horses, chariots, gleaming armor, and shining weapons. He moved in with the Roman army at the beginning of the Passover festival week to make sure that nothing got out of hand at this time when the Hebrew people remembered their deliverance from Pharaoh in Egypt twelve hundred years before. Insurrection was in the air, along with enlarged hopes that God would come and rescue them from Rome's oppression.

From the east, from the Mount of Olives, came the second procession, a commoner's procession. Jesus wore an ordinary robe, brandishing no weapons and riding on a donkey. Matthew and Mark tell us what was going on in people's minds: the prophecy of Zechariah was coming true, the coming of a different kind of Messiah/King, a king of peace: "Lo, your king is coming victorious yet humble riding on a donkey. He shall banish chariot . . . and war horse . . . and warrior's bow. And he shall command peace to the nations" (Zechariah 9:9-10 [my translation]).

As Jesus entered the Eastern Gate, throngs of people were there to greet him. They waved palms and spread their garments on the road. Some sang, "Hosanna! Blessed is the one who comes in the name of the Lord!" (Mark 11:9, NRSV). Luke records some saying, "Blessed is the *king* who comes in the name of the Lord" (Luke 19:38, NRSV [emphasis added]). Some asked, "Who is this?" Others replied, "This is the prophet Jesus from Nazareth in Galilee" (Matthew 21:10-11, NRSV).

"Who was he?" we still ask. Prophet, king, messiah? Some combination of these? Author and historical Jesus scholar Paula Fredriksen says that the term *messiah* had varied meanings in Jesus' time: "a priest, a prophet, a royal warrior, perhaps even an angelic, non-human figure."[2] Jesus was transforming the meaning of Messiah as he rode into town.

In Luke's account, Jesus' followers were making such a glorious fuss that some Pharisees told Jesus, "Teacher, order them to stop." Jesus replied, "I tell you, if these were silent, the very stones would cry out" (Luke 19:40).

Was Jesus a king? He had refused Satan's temptation in the wilderness to make him a political king over the nations (Luke 4:5-8). He had fled from the crowd that, after a miracle he performed, was about to take him by force and make him king (John 6:14-15). On these days he could have been made such a king, but he would not.

God was the ruler of the kingdom that Jesus preached. And the kingdom was counter to all the kingdoms of the world. At Jesus' trial in John's Gospel, Jesus said clearly, "My kingship is not of this world; if my kingship were of this world, my servants would fight, that I not be handed over" (John 18:36).

Was Jesus the Messiah? The word *messiah* means "anointed one," and he surely was anointed by the Spirit of God. Did he fit the many and varied hopes of the Jewish people about the Messiah? No, he didn't. Reality was not transfigured into a perfect realm of peace, mercy, justice, and joy with his coming. He would be a suffering Messiah, bringing in God's time the healing of God.

Was he a prophet? As an earlier chapter suggests that surely he was (although also more than a prophet). He wept over Jerusalem and offered this prophetic lament: "If you, even you, had only recognized on this day the things that make for peace! But now they are hidden from your eyes" (Luke 19:42).

And then he prophesied that the city would be destroyed. In Matthew's Gospel he offers another prophetic lament:

> O Jerusalem, Jerusalem, killing the prophets and stoning those who are sent to you! How often would I have gathered your children together as a hen gathers her brood under her wings, and you would not! Behold, your house is forsaken and desolate. (Matthew 23:37-38)

Such was the pathos of the Prophet. No wonder there were those who wanted him dead!

THE TEMPLE INCIDENT

Perhaps the one action that most led to Jesus' death was his prophetic action in the temple. Mark places the incident on Monday, immediately after the entry into Jerusalem. Jesus had gone to look at the temple on Sunday, and then he retired for the night in Bethany with his disciples.

In the morning, Jesus entered the temple and drove out the money changers and turned over their tables. The money changers helped people buy the animals for sacrifice in the temple. As he drove the money changers and their animals out, Jesus said, "Is it not written, 'My house shall be called a house of prayer for all the nations'? But you have made it a den of robbers" (Mark 11:17, NRSV). It was a prophetic action and sign, a powerful symbolic act that challenged the temple leadership and ruling elite. They had forgotten the meaning of Torah and were in collusion with Rome.

Even in his own time, Jesus was not alone in this critique. The sentiment was widespread, expressed with special force by the Essene community at the Dead Sea. Corruption and collusion had delegitimized the first-century temple leadership.

Jesus' protest was not anti-Jewish. It was *deeply* Jewish. He was trying to purify his faith tradition and save it from destruction.

Jesus was quoting from Isaiah: "My house shall be called a house of prayer for all peoples" (Isaiah 56:7, NRSV). It was the vision of the perfected temple of God to which all the nations would flow, including foreigners, eunuchs, and outcasts (Isaiah 56:4-8).

And Jesus' words echoed the prophet Jeremiah, who had charged that the temple of his day had become corrupt, a den of thieves. The ancient prophet's judgment was broad:

Thus says the LORD of hosts, the God of Israel: Amend your ways and your doings, and let me dwell with you in this place. Do not trust in these deceptive words: "This is the temple of the LORD, the temple of the LORD, the temple of the LORD." For if you truly amend your ways and your doings, if you truly act justly one with another, if you do not oppress the alien, the orphan, and the widow, or shed innocent blood in this place, and if you do not go after other gods to your own hurt, then I will dwell with you in this place. . . . Has this house, which is called by my name, become a den of robbers in your sight? (Jeremiah 7:3-11, NRSV)

In good prophetic fashion, Jesus was attacking worship detached from right living, the collusion of the power elite with Rome, and a social order disordered by oppression and injustice.

Such an action in the temple during Passover week most surely got the attention of both the religious and the political leaders. It was like a protest at the U.S. Capitol, the National Cathedral, and Wall Street all rolled into one.

PROPHESYING THE DESTRUCTION OF THE TEMPLE

Jesus went even further than his action in the temple. He prophesied the destruction of the temple. We read it in Mark's Gospel:

As he came out of the temple, one of his disciples said to him, "Look, Teacher, what large stones and what large buildings!" Then Jesus asked him, "Do you see these great buildings? Not one stone will be left here upon another; all will be thrown down." (Mark 13:1-2, NRSV)

In John's account, after the cleansing of the temple, Jesus said, "Destroy [that is, *you* destroy] this temple, and in three days I will raise it up" (John 2:19).

Memory of Jesus' words would be used in some fashion against him at his trial. Here is how Mark reported it:

> Some stood and gave false testimony against him, saying, "We heard him say, 'I will destroy the temple that is made with hands, and in three days I will build another, not made with hands.'" But even on this point their testimony did not agree. (Mark 14:57-59, NRSV)

What did Jesus actually say, and what did he mean by what he said? We cannot be sure. Again, what we have in the Gospels is "the history of the memory" of the first followers.

Jesus could have been prophesying what *did* happen in 70 CE. Zealot attempts to overthrow the Roman occupation provoked Emperor Vespasian to send the full fury of the Roman legions against Jerusalem. As the Jewish historian Josephus described it, there were almost three million Jews in Jerusalem gathered for Passover when the attack came. And 1,332,490 Jews died. As many as five hundred were crucified as a public spectacle. Some ninety-seven thousand were sold into slavery, so that in Alexandria a slave was sold for less than a goat. The temple was stormed and burned to the ground. A sheet of fire covered the entire Temple Mount.

It may be impossible to fathom the horror of that calamity for the Jews. It was a spiritual crisis too. How could God allow this to happen to the chosen people and God's own beloved city? Did Jesus see this terrible event as inevitable, given the social, spiritual, and political conditions of his day?

Or, to pose an alternative, did Jesus see the coming kingdom bringing a good catastrophe, a "eucatastrophe" (to use the word coined by J. R. R. Tolkien)? Historical existence would be ended as we know it, and there would come a new heaven and earth, a new Jerusalem and a new temple.

We cannot know the precise turning of Jesus' mind—other than his complete trust in God's power and desire to bring a kingdom good beyond imagining and with it the healing of the world. Whatever Jesus meant, his words were used against him at his trial.

THE ANOINTING AT BETHANY

In the midst of the terrors of the week, the Gospels report a beautiful private scene.[3] Jesus was in Bethany, a few miles from Jerusalem, in the home of Simon the leper. A woman broke into the company of family and friends. (John's Gospel places the scene at the home of Mary, Martha, and Lazarus, with Mary being the woman with the oil.) She took an alabaster flask of rare ointment and poured it on Jesus' head, in the way that kings were anointed.

Some of Jesus' disciples were indignant: "Why the waste?" The ointment, they said, could have been sold for a large sum that could have been given to the poor. Jesus replied:

> Let her alone; why do you trouble her? She has done a beautiful thing to me. For you always have the poor with you, and whenever you will, you can do good to them; but you will not always have me. She has done what she could; she has anointed my body beforehand for burying. And truly, I say to you, wherever the gospel is preached in the whole world, what she has done will be told in memory of her. (Mark 14:6-9)

This woman had the gift of *recognition*. She knew who Jesus was and what was going to happen to him. Hers was an extravagant act of devotion. The male disciples were still in denial. The women around Jesus would stick with him to and through the end. The male disciples would desert him and flee.

CONFLICT IN JERUSALEM

During the last week of Jesus' life there were a number of confrontations between him and his opponents. Perhaps the most memorable was a question concerning taxes to Caesar (see Matthew 22:15-22; Mark 12:13-17; Luke 20:20-26).

Two groups, the Pharisees and the Herodians, both protectors of the social order, came to Jesus to "trap" him. After some introductory flattery, they posed this question: "Is it lawful to pay taxes to Caesar?"

It was a loaded question in an incendiary week. The Jewish people hated the Roman oppression and the taxes that Rome imposed. Some said that it was spiritually unlawful for a Jew to pay taxes to Caesar.

If Jesus said yes, he would be seen as a collaborator with Rome; if he said no, he would be a dangerous seditionist.

Jesus' response was brilliant. He asked to see a denarius, on which was stamped an image of Caesar's head and his title as "Son of God." Some said that the very title was blasphemous, and so they refused to even carry the coins. Jesus then said, "Render therefore to Caesar the things that are Caesar's, and to God the things that are God's" (Matthew 22:21).

He turned the question back to them as with a mirror. What *does* belong to Caesar and what to God? You must decide. Jesus let them work out the calculus. He escaped the trap of being seen as a collaborator or insurrectionist. He would later be seen as an enemy of the state, but in fact he belonged to no party.

NOTES

1. Marcus Borg and John Dominic Crossan, *The Last Week: The Day-by-Day Account of Jesus' Final Week in Jerusalem* (San Francisco: HarperSanFrancisco, 2006), 2–5.

2. Paula Fredriksen, *Jesus of Nazareth, King of the Jews: A Jewish Life and the Emergence of Christianity* (New York: Knopf, 1999), 212.

3. A parallel anointing scene is found in Matthew 26:6-13; Mark 14:3-9; John 12:1-8. Luke 7:36-50 records a different anointing.

23

THE LAST NIGHT AND DAY

On Thursday of his final week, Jesus had his last meal with his disciples. In John's Gospel, we are told that on that night, Jesus took a towel and washed his disciples' feet, taking on the role of a servant. And he gave them a new commandment: "A new commandment I give to you, that you love one another; even as I have loved you, that you also love one another" (John 13:34).

THE LAST MEAL

In Matthew, Mark, and Luke, the emphasis is on the sharing of the bread and wine. In Mark's Gospel, we read:

> While they were eating, he took a loaf of bread, and after blessing it he broke it, gave it to them, and said, "Take; this is my body." Then he took the cup, and after giving thanks he gave it to them, and all of them drank from it. He said to them, "This is my blood of the covenant, which is poured out for many. Truly I tell you, I will never again drink of the fruit of the wine until that day when I drink it new in the kingdom of God. (Mark 14:22-25, NRSV)

"This is my body, which is *given* for you," is how Luke recorded the words (Luke 22:19, NRSV [emphasis added]). The bread and cup represent Jesus' whole life, *given*, *poured out*, for others, from the first day until now, standing in the shadow of the cross.

The words that Jesus spoke at the table that night are remembered with slight differences in the Gospels and in Paul (see Matthew 26:26-28; Mark 14:22-24; Luke 22:19-20; 1 Corinthians 11:23-26), but the force of the words is the same. The bread and wine stand for Jesus' life and his full giving of self for others. The meanings are inexhaustible. Jesus was foretelling his death and linking that death with God's redemption of the world. His life was being *given*, not demanded, for Israel, for his followers, for the world.

THE GARDEN

After the supper, Jesus went to the garden of Gethsemane and prayed to God:

> *Abba, Father, all things are possible to you.*
> *Remove this cup from me!*
> *Yet, not what I want, but what you want.*
> (Mark 14:36 [my translation])

He prayed to *Abba*. He prayed in agony. He prayed to be spared, for God's redemptive work to be accomplished in some other way. But he traveled through that agony to a place of trust in God and acceptance for whatever was to come.

Then Judas entered the garden and betrayed Jesus. According to plan, he kissed Jesus to identify him for the Jewish and Roman soldiers who accompanied him. They arrested Jesus and led him to what would be his first trial.

THE TRIALS

The first trial, or interrogation, was before Caiaphas the high priest and an ad hoc council of Jewish leaders. Accusations came before the council that Mark called "false witness." Some sought to use Jesus' words about the destruction of the temple against him. But as Mark concludes, "their testimony did not agree" (Mark 14:59). Caiaphas then asked Jesus, "Are you the Messiah, the son of the Blessed One?" In Mark's Gospel, Jesus answered forthrightly: "I am." In Matthew and Luke, he answers more elusively, "You say so."

Caiaphas then tore his garments as the official response to what he heard as blasphemy. As far as Caiaphas was concerned, Jesus had blasphemed by taking upon himself the messianic title. Under Jewish law, blasphemy was an act punishable by stoning. But the Jewish leaders under Roman control did not have the power to order an execution. So they handed Jesus over to Pilate, the Roman governor.

Pilate was a ruthless man famous for his acts of terror on behalf of Rome. "Are you the king of the Jews?" Pilate asked. Anyone claiming to be the Messiah or a king would be a threat to Roman control. Jesus replied, "You say that I am a king." Then, when Jesus told Pilate that he came into the world to testify to the truth, Pilate asked, "What is truth?" Pilate was looking truth in the eyes but did not see it.

Pilate then offered those gathered around in the palace courtyard the option of choosing to release either Jesus or a convicted seditionist, Barabbas. The crowd cried out for Jesus' death, "Crucify him!" This crowd was not the multitude that sang praises and waved palms at the triumphal entry. The crowd cannot be identified with the Jewish people in general. They were a smaller group gathered in the palace courtyard, allowed in by the powers that be.

Rome could not abide a man who could be perceived as king of the Jews, even if he himself did not claim to be so. The Jewish leaders were paranoid about this man whose popularity and power might inspire an uprising and upset the fragile state of things.

In John's Gospel, Caiaphas puts their logic plainly: "You do not understand that it is expedient for you that one man should die for the people, and that the whole nation should not perish" (John 11:50). It is the "logic" of what theologian René Girard calls the mechanism of "sacred violence," which stands close to the heart of both politics and religion; if a scapegoat is killed, the nation will be saved.

After the trial came the brutal scourging of Jesus with whips and the mockery of Jesus' supposed kingship by placing a royal purple robe on him and pushing a crown of thorns onto his head.

Jesus was made to carry the crossbeam of the cross on which he was to be executed through the streets of Jerusalem, outside the wall to the place called Golgotha, the Place of the Skull. At one point, weakened by the whipping, he crumpled under the weight of the crossbeam, and a man named Simon of Cyrene carried it for him.

When they reached the place of execution, Jesus' hands were nailed to the crossbeam, which was then fastened to the vertical beam. His feet were nailed to that beam, and he was lifted up to die.

It was a horrendous form of execution reserved for the worst offenders against the Roman state. Those crucified often took an excruciatingly long time to die. Scavenging birds picked at the carcass, and then the remains were thrown in a heap on the ground to rot and be eaten by dogs or vermin.

On Jesus' cross Pilate had inscribed the words "King of the Jews," a mocking title; and it was also a warning: this is what happens to would-be kings. People came by and taunted Jesus: "He saved others; he cannot save himself." "Let the Messiah, the king of Israel, come down from the cross now, so that we may see and believe." But a Roman centurion, standing at the foot of the cross, said, "Surely this man was the Son of God." The centurion recognized that his own king, Caesar, though worshiped as the Son of God, was not, and that Jesus was.

On the cross, while dying, Jesus uttered what are known as the "seven last words," words that truly displayed his character. Novelist Flannery O'Connor wrote, "The man in the violent situation reveals those qualities least dispensable in his personality, those qualities which are all he will have to take into eternity with him."[1] In the violent situation of the cross, Jesus uttered these four statements (not in this particular order):

1. "I thirst" (John 19:28), the cry of a fully human man in the process of dying.
2. "Truly, I say to you, today you will dwell with me in Paradise" (Luke 23:43), his words to a thief on the cross next to his who wanted to be remembered when Jesus came into his kingdom.
3. "Woman, behold your son! . . . [Son,] behold your mother!" (John 19:26-27), offering his mother into the care of the disciple whom Jesus loved, and the disciple into her care.
4. "It is finished" (John 19:30), the last "word" in John's Gospel, meaning both "It is over" and "It is completed."

And, as described in chapter 17, Jesus prayed three prayers from the cross:

1. *The prayer of forgiveness*: "Father, forgive them, for they know not what they do" (Luke 23:34). This astounding, seemingly impossible prayer has created a forgiveness community stretching over two thousand years, from the martyr Stephen, who echoed these words while he was being killed (Acts 7:60), to Martin Luther King Jr., who said that we must love our enemies. For there is, King said, something good in the worst of us and some evil in the best of us.[2]
2. *The prayer of abandonment*: "Eli, Eli, lama sabachthani? . . . My God, my God, why have you forsaken me?" (Matthew 27:46), a quotation from Psalm 22:1.

At that moment, Jesus identified himself with God's people through the centuries who had suffered and felt abandoned by God, yet still, as the psalm goes on to express, had trust in God. It is a terrible cry. Did he *feel* abandoned by God, his *Abba*?

3. *The prayer of relinquishment*: "Father, into your hands I commit my spirit" (Luke 23:46). Here was the full yielding of himself into the hands of God, the supreme letting go, which is faith at its most profound. These words recited the beloved nighttime prayer offered by Hebrew girls and boys, men and women, through the centuries, from Psalm 31:5.

In the violent situation of the cross, Jesus' personality shone through his words. Here was a man of faith, compassion, and mercy who forgave his killers, opened paradise to a thief, took care of his mother, and was willing to trust his life utterly into the hands of God. As the nonviolent son/servant of God, Jesus was willing to die by the sword rather than kill by the sword no matter how just the cause.

Around the cross were women, Mary Magdalene and several others who had followed Jesus from Galilee. The male disciples were nowhere to be found, except for the disciple whom Jesus loved, known from John's Gospel. Judas had betrayed Jesus; Peter, under questioning on Thursday night, had denied even knowing him, and the others had just fled.

Joseph of Arimathea, a man of means and a respected member of the Sanhedrin, the Jewish council, bravely went to Pilate and asked for Jesus' body so he could be given a respectful burial. Pilate agreed, and after confirming that Jesus was dead, Pilate let Joseph take Jesus from the cross, wrap his body in linen cloth, and lay him in Joseph's burial tomb. Mary Magdalene and Mary the mother of Jesus were present at the burial.

What was the hope any of them had? Perhaps they took hope in the words of Wisdom, a sacred book written between the Testaments that spoke of the fate of righteous martyrs during the Maccabean revolt:

> But the souls of the righteous are in the hand of God, and no torment will ever touch them. In the eyes of the foolish they seem to have died, and their departure was thought to be a disaster, and their going from us to be their destruction; but they are at peace. For though in the sight of others they were punished, their hope is full of immortality. (Wisdom 3:1-4, NRSV)

Did they remember Jesus' words about rising again? Did they hope in some general resurrection of all the dead that would happen soon? Could they feel such hope in the midst of the crushing grief? We cannot know.

The life of the historical Jesus was ended. Saturday the Sabbath came and went. Mary Magdalene and a few other women prepared spices to anoint Jesus' body. What happened next would supersede all expectation, change the course of humanity, and bring to birth a new faith.

NOTE

1. Flannery O'Connor, "On Her Own Work," cited by Andre Dubus, *The Times Are Never So Bad: A Novella and Eight Short Stories* (Boston: David R. Godine, 1983), frontispiece.

2. Martin Luther King Jr. "Loving Your Enemies" (sermon, Dexter Avenue Baptist Church, Montgomery, AL, December, 1957).

24

THE RESURRECTION: FIVE ACCOUNTS

What happened at the resurrection of Jesus? Whatever happened changed everything. No resurrection, no Christianity. The resurrection happened in history; it was a historical event, although it cannot be proven by modern historical tools. There were no video cameras (what would a video camera have captured?), and all the eyewitnesses to the resurrection events in the Gospels were followers of Jesus. What would an outsider have experienced?

None of the Gospels describe the actual resurrection itself. What we have in the Gospels are (1) four different accounts of an empty tomb on Sunday, the third day; and (2) three different collections of reports of appearances of the Risen Christ, or more-than-historical Jesus. (Mark's Gospel is the exception to #2; see below.)

We begin with a review of the chronology of the resurrection accounts in the New Testament. The apostle Paul's experience of the Risen Christ happened last, around eighteen months after Jesus' death, but his written account of the resurrection appearances is the first, or earliest, around 50 CE.

The book of Acts describes what happened to the man who would become known as the apostle Paul. "Breathing threats and murder against the disciples of the Lord" (Acts

9:1), Paul, who at that time was named Saul, was on his way to Damascus to persecute the believers there. On his way, light flashed from heaven, and Saul heard a voice saying, "Saul, Saul, why do you persecute me?"

"Who are you, Lord?" Saul replied. The voice said, "I am Jesus, whom you are persecuting. Rise and enter the city, and you will be told what to do." Those around Saul "stood speechless because they had heard the voice but saw no one" (Acts 9:7, NRSV).

The implication is that in the bright, blinding mystery of the light, Saul saw the Risen Christ and heard him. And seeing him, he could see no more. He was led by the hand to Damascus, where a Christian named Ananias would lay hands on him. Saul's eyes would be opened again to see. And he would hear Jesus' words through Ananias: the Risen One's call to him to be an apostle to the Gentiles. (At some point between that encounter on the road to Damascus in Acts 9 and his subsequent ministry with another disciple named Barnabas, Saul became known as Paul, a sobriquet first mentioned in Acts 13:9.)

In his Letter to the Galatians, Paul would call what happened an "apocalypse," a "revelation," of Jesus Christ (Galatians 1:12). Later, writing to the Corinthians, he called it an "appearance" (1 Corinthians 15:8). "Have I not seen Jesus our Lord?" he asked rhetorically (1 Corinthians 9:1). Then, in 1 Corinthians 15, he passed along what had been passed on to him, an early Easter creed citing a series of resurrection appearances:

> that he was raised on the third day . . . and that he appeared to Cephas [Peter], then to the twelve. Then he appeared to more than five hundred brothers and sisters at one time, most of whom are still alive. . . . Then he appeared to James, then to all the apostles. Last of all, as to one untimely born, he appeared also to me. (1 Corinthians 15:4-8, NRSV)

That is the earliest written account we have of the resurrection, in the early 50s CE.

The Gospel of Mark was written in the 70s CE, Matthew and Luke in the 80s, and John in the 90s. So there was a considerable time between the death of Jesus around 30 CE and these writings. The resurrection stories had passed through oral tradition and pamphlet-sized collections before becoming part of the Gospels as we have them.

Matthew and Luke had Mark as their major source. John appears to have been formed in a stream of tradition independent of Matthew, Mark, and Luke. So what we have in the Gospels are resurrection stories written forty to sixty years after Jesus' death.

Many works on the historical Jesus give scant attention to the resurrection because it lies beyond the reach of modern historical investigation. I choose to offer a fuller treatment. The appearances of Jesus were historical events with historical consequences, even though they lie beyond historical proving.[1] The more-than-historical Jesus extends the story of Jesus beyond his death.

I will offer a panorama of the four different Gospel accounts of what happened that changed everything. As I do, we can ponder their likenesses and their differences.

RESURRECTION BY MARK

Mark's Gospel has the shortest resurrection account, just eight verses in Mark 16. The earliest version of the Gospel ends so abruptly that the second-century church added some verses to make it "complete." Here is how Mark tells the Easter story.

When the Sabbath (Saturday) was over, Mary Magdalene, Mary the mother of James, and Salome prepared spices to anoint Jesus' body in the tomb. Early Sunday morning, when the sun had just risen, they arrived at the tomb. They had wondered en route who would help them move the large stone at the door of the tomb so they could go inside.

When they got there, they saw that the stone was already rolled back. Entering the tomb, they saw a young man "dressed in white" (an angel?) and were struck with amazement. Here was something beyond normal happening. The Greek word for "amazed" (*ekthambeō*) stands for something much stronger than casual surprise or even shock. Other translators use words and phrases, such as *dumbfounded, bewildered, terrified, alarmed, taken aback, astonished, scared out of their skin.*

The young man said to the women, "Do not be amazed," and then he continued: "You seek Jesus of Nazareth, who was crucified. He has risen, he is not here; see the place where they laid him" (Mark 16:6).

So we have an empty tomb and a young man/messenger in white speaking to them and showing it to them. Next, the young man gave a commission: "Go, tell his disciples and Peter that he is going before you to Galilee; there you will see him" (Mark 16:7).

What do the women do? Here is how the earliest manuscript ends the Gospel: "So they went out and fled from the tomb; for terror and amazement had seized them; and they said nothing to anyone, for they were afraid" (Mark 16:8, NRSV).

It seems an odd way to end a Gospel (*euangelion*, good news). Some posit that the ending of Mark's Gospel was broken off at the end of the scroll, where wear and tear were the greatest, and lost. We could call it the "Unfinished Gospel." The early Christian community thought so, for they later added twelve verses (Mark 16:9-20) that were a compilation of Easter stories circulating at the time.

What we *can* say is that without something else happening, the Jesus Story might have stopped there—with terrified women afraid to tell what had happened at the open tomb. That something else, or something more, were appearances of the Risen Christ to followers. "Jesus is going ahead of you! Follow him until you meet him!" Here is where the Unfinished Gospel ends. We are to finish the Gospel ourselves. Matthew tells us what happened next.

RESURRECTION BY MATTHEW

Matthew 28 begins with two women (not three), Mary Magdalene and "the other Mary" going to the tomb. Then an earthquake happened, and an angel (not a young man) descended and rolled back the tomb. "His appearance was like lightning, and his clothing white as snow" (Matthew 28:3, NRSV).

The Roman guards who were sent there to guard the tomb trembled and fainted "like dead men." Matthew's Gospel is the only one to have Roman soldiers present. It is a thrilling symbolic moment: Jesus is alive, while representatives of imperial Rome lie on the ground as dead men.

Then the angel spoke the same message as in Mark's Gospel: "Do not be afraid. He is not here, he is risen. Come see where he lay." Then they gave the same commission: "Go tell the disciples that he is risen. He will go to Galilee. You can meet him there."

In this Gospel the women went out "in fear and great joy." And in this Gospel they ran to tell the disciples. Now comes the new moment in the resurrection story, going beyond Mark's ending. The risen Jesus appeared to them and said, "Greetings!" They took hold of his feet and "worshiped" him. Then Jesus gave to them the commission himself: "Do not be afraid; go and tell my brothers to go to Galilee; there they will see me" (Matthew 28:10, NRSV).

We are not given details about what Jesus' "resurrection body" looked like. Paul would call it a *sōma pneumatikon*, a "spiritual body," not a ghost, not a resuscitated corpse, but something else.

Matthew's resurrection story ends with the disciples in Galilee on a mountain. (Matthew's Gospel loves mountains for important moments.) Jesus appeared to them there. The text says, "When they saw him, they worshiped him; but some doubted" (Matthew 28:17, NRSV). An honest account.

The nature of Jesus' resurrection appearance was startling enough, ambiguous and mysterious enough that it did not automatically create faith from the disciples. Revelation is always a divine-human dance. God takes the lead, but we must follow. We might think that if the risen Christ were to appear to us, we would automatically believe, but it was not so with the disciples and would not likely be so for us.

Jesus then gave them what is called the Great Commission:

> Go therefore and make disciples of all nations, baptizing them in the name of the Father and of the Son and of the Holy Spirit, and teaching them to obey everything that I have commanded you. And remember, I am with you always, to the end of the age. (Matthew 28:19-20, NRSV)

Matthew's Gospel begins with the proclamation of the Christ child being "Immanuel," God-with-us (Matthew 1:23), and ends with Jesus' promise to be with us forever.

The more-than-historical Jesus was offering a worldwide commission broader than the historical Jesus could have given. The precise wording, especially as found in the baptismal formula—"in the name of the Father and of the Son and of the Holy Spirit"—appears to have been the augmentation of the Christian community during the fifty years between Jesus' death and the writing of Matthew's Gospel. They had the conviction that the more-than-historical Jesus was still speaking. As Gracie Allen is credited with saying, "Never place a period where God has placed a comma!"

RESURRECTION BY LUKE

Luke begins his Easter story (Luke 24) similarly to Mark and Matthew: some women came to the tomb, bringing spices. They found the tomb empty, went in, and did not see the body. While they were "perplexed" (NRSV) by this oddity, suddenly two men (not one, not identified as angels) in dazzlingly bright clothes appeared. The women "were terrified and bowed their faces to the ground"; the men said to them, "Why do you look for the living among the dead? He is not here, but has risen" (Luke 24:5, NRSV).

Some of the women are identified by name: Mary Magdalene, Joanna, Mary the mother of James, as well as "the other women" who had traveled with Jesus from Galilee. The women ran to tell the eleven disciples what had happened.

The men did not receive the women's news with joy and unmixed faith. Quite the opposite: "But these words seemed to them an idle tale, and they did not believe them" (Luke 24:11, NRSV). Peter, however, ran to the tomb to see for himself, saw the burial clothes lying in the tomb, and "wondered" what had happened.

Next we have the story unique to Luke about two disciples on that Easter Sunday, trudging their way sadly from Jerusalem to Emmaus.[2] They talked with each other about what had happened during the last days. Suddenly Jesus appeared and began to walk beside them, but they did not recognize him.

Jesus the stranger asked, "What are you talking about as you walk along?" One of them, Cleopas, said, "Are you the only stranger in Jerusalem who does not know what things have taken place there in these days?" (Jesus was the only one who *did* know!) He asked them, deadpan, "What things?"

They told him about Jesus, his life and his death, and then spoke sad words of grief: "We had hoped that he was the one to redeem Israel" (Luke 24:21, NRSV). "We had hoped. . . ." Then they told Jesus about the Sunday morning happenings, the empty tomb, the angels, the women. They seemed unconvinced. Jesus told them, "Oh, how foolish you are, and how slow at heart to believe all that the prophets have declared! Was it not necessary that the Messiah should suffer these things and enter into his glory?" (Luke 24:25-26, NRSV).

It was not obvious; a *suffering* Messiah seemed an impossible contradiction in terms. Then Jesus opened the Scriptures to them and talked about Moses and the prophets, interpreting the things about himself in Hebrew Scripture. Still they did not recognize him.

They traveled on in the sunset of their grief until dusk, when they reached Emmaus. Jesus acted as if he was going on, but they compelled him to spend the night. "Stay with us," they said.

That evening at dinner, Jesus the guest suddenly became the host. He took bread, blessed it and broke it, and gave it to the disciples. Suddenly their eyes were opened, and they recognized who he was—and just as suddenly Jesus disappeared from their sight.

They looked back with 20/20 spiritual hindsight then and said, "Were not our hearts burning within us while he was talking to us on the road, while he was opening the scriptures to us?" (Luke 24:32, NRSV).

The joyful mystery of Easter deepens. Jesus appeared unrecognized. He walked and talked Scripture with them. Still he was unrecognized. Only as he broke the bread did they recognize him. (He had done so just like this so often!) Then he suddenly disappeared. His body was unrecognized, then recognized, then disappeared. Here, again, was not a resuscitated corpse. It was a different kind of body, not bound by normal space and time.

The two disciples returned to Jerusalem to the Eleven, who announced what they already knew: "The Lord has risen." The others described how the Lord had appeared to Peter. Then the two told what had happened to them at Emmaus.

While they were talking, the risen Jesus suddenly appeared in their midst and said, "*Shalom*, peace be with you." They were "startled and terrified, and thought that they were seeing a ghost" (Luke 24:37, NRSV). Jesus said to them, "Why are you frightened? Why the doubts? Look at my hands and feet, touch and see that I'm not a ghost" (Luke 24:38-39 [my translation]). The text says that they were joyful, disbelieving, and wondering all at the same time.

Then Jesus asked, "Do you have anything to eat?" So they gave him some broiled fish and he ate. In this detail, Luke emphasizes the nonghostly, "physical" presence of Jesus in his resurrection body.

Jesus then once more interpreted Scripture for disciples. He interprets the *whole* of Hebrew Scripture—the Law, the Prophets, the Writings. Luke also emphasizes how what happened to Jesus in the death and resurrection was a fulfillment of Hebrew Scripture.

Then Jesus commissioned them—a common theme in all the Gospels: preach repentance and the forgiveness of sins to all the nations. "You are my witnesses." He also told them to stay in Jerusalem until they were "clothed with power from on high." Luke, who wrote Acts as well, will explain that this happened at Pentecost, fifty days after the resurrection.

Finally, Jesus led them to Bethany, and lifting up his hands, he blessed them and then withdrew from them into heaven, what the church calls the ascension. The disciples returned with great joy to Jerusalem—like the great joy experienced at Jesus' birth in Luke. Luke concludes, "And they were continually in the temple blessing God" (Luke 24:53, NRSV). The Christian church's painful break with Judaism would not happen for decades.

So we see in Luke a set of stories of the resurrection happening, not in Galilee as Matthew tells it, but in and around Jerusalem. Luke's emphasis on the Scripture (our Old Testament) conveys the message that when it comes to God's work in history and in Jesus, *all stories are one story*. It is also important to note that only the resurrection appearance opens their eyes to all these connections.

RESURRECTION BY JOHN

John begins his resurrection account with Mary Magdalene alone at the tomb in John 20. When she saw that the stone of the tomb had been removed, she ran to tell Peter and the "other disciple" (that is, the Beloved Disciple). She did not fathom anything like resurrection: "They have taken the Lord out of the tomb, and we do not know where they have laid him" (John 20:2).

Peter and the other disciple ran to the tomb. The Beloved Disciple got there first, and he peered into the tomb but did not go in. Peter went on in and saw the linens lying there. The other disciple followed Peter into the tomb. He "saw and believed." Then they returned to their homes.

Mary Magdalene was now alone in the garden where the tomb was. She was weeping. As she wept, she bent to look into the tomb and saw two angels (two as in Luke, angels as in Matthew) in white, sitting where the body of Jesus once lay. They said, "Woman, why are you weeping?" Mary replied,

"They've taken away my Lord, and I do not know where they have laid him" (John 20:13, NRSV).

Then suddenly Jesus appeared. Mary saw him but did not recognize him. "Why are you weeping?" Jesus asked. Supposing he was the gardener, she said, "Sir, if you have carried him away, tell me where you have laid him, and I will take him away" (John 20:15, NRSV).

Then Jesus spoke her name, "Mary," and she turned and cried out, "Rabbouni, my dear Master." She recognized him by the sound of his voice as he called her name.

Jesus responded, "Do not hold onto me. I am ascending to my Father. Go tell the disciples I am ascending to my Father and your Father, my God and your God."

Mary obeyed Jesus' call, running and announcing to the disciples, "I have seen the Lord," and told them what had happened. Because of this scene, Thomas Aquinas gave Mary the title "Apostle to the Apostles."

The second scene in John's Easter story happened in a house in Jerusalem. It was Sunday evening. The disciples were huddled in fear behind locked doors. What would happen to them now?

Jesus suddenly appeared and said, "Peace be with you." Then he showed them his hands and side. When they realized who he was, they rejoiced.

A second time Jesus said, "Peace be with you." Perhaps their guilty consciences needed to hear the forgiveness of the peace twice.

Then Jesus commissioned them: "As the Father has sent me, so send I you." Then he breathed his breath on them and said, "Receive the Holy Spirit." He told them what they were to do: go and loose people from their sins. (Recall that the Greek word for "forgiveness" means literally "to loose.") God's grace forgives and sets us free. It is pardon and power.

One of Jesus' disciples, Thomas, was not with them that night. Upon hearing what had happened, he said, "Unless I see the mark of the nails in his hands and put my finger in the mark of the nails and my hand in his side, I will not believe"

(John 20:25, NRSV). Poet Denise Levertov places these words in Thomas's mouth: "I needed blood to tell me the truth."[3]

A week later, the disciples were gathered at the house, this time with Thomas present. The Risen Christ appeared again and said, "*Shalom*, peace." Then he invited Thomas, "Put your finger here and see my hands. Reach out your hand and put it in my side. Do not doubt but believe" (John 20:27, NRSV). Jesus did not begrudge Thomas his "obstinate need," as Levertov puts it.

Thomas responded, "My Lord and my God!"—a supreme confession of faith. We do not know whether he actually touched Jesus' wounds, but *believing* happened.

There is one more story, in John 21, this one at the Sea of Galilee. Peter and the disciples, seven of them all told, had gone back to fishing. Just after daybreak, Jesus appeared on the shore. They did not recognize him. (Nonrecognition of the Risen Christ is seen in Luke's Emmaus story and in John's scene with Jesus and Mary in the garden.) "Boys, caught anything?" he asked like a curious vacationer. "No," they answered. And he said, "Cast your nets on the other side." They did so, and the nets were so full that the men could not haul them into the boat. This episode echoes Luke's version of the call of the disciples to follow Jesus (Luke 5:4-11). Jesus is calling them anew!

The Beloved Disciple exclaimed to Peter, "It is the Lord!"

Peter couldn't wait for the boat to make land. He jumped overboard and thrashed his way to shore. The other disciples followed in the boat, dragging their nets behind them.

When they got to shore, there was a charcoal fire glowing, and Jesus was cooking breakfast for them. He shared the bread and fish.

After the meal, Peter found himself alone with Jesus. Jesus said, "Simon, son of John, do you love me more than these?"

Peter said, "Yes, Lord, you know that I love you."

Jesus said, "Feed my lambs."

A second time Jesus asked, "Simon, son of John, do you love me?"

"Yes, Lord, you know that I love you," Peter answered.

Jesus told him, "Tend my sheep."

Then a third time Jesus asked, "Simon, son of John, do you love me?"

At the third time Peter was struck to the heart. He had denied Jesus three times around a charcoal fire on Thursday night, the night of Jesus' arrest. Now around a morning campfire he was being asked to declare his love three times.

"Lord, you know everything," Peter answered. "You know I love you."

"Feed my sheep," Jesus answered.

Then Jesus made plain his new commissioning to Peter. "Follow me," he said, just as he had said on that first day they met.

John closes the Gospel by declaring that if all the things Jesus did were written down, all the libraries of the world could not contain them. The works of the more-than-historical Jesus march on through history.

RESURRECTION: SUMMARY THOUGHTS

There are a number of differences among the Gospel resurrection stories. Did the appearances first happen in Galilee or Jerusalem? Was there one man or two? Was it an angel (or angels) or not? How many women were at the tomb? The list could go on. Each of the Gospels has its own set of resurrection appearance stories too. We see four streams of traditions—five, counting Paul—that developed independently. The church chose to include all four Gospels, even with their discrepancies. It chose to honor diversity within the unity of the telling of the Jesus Story.

Amid the differences there are several important commonalities:

1. the empty tomb on the third day;
2. appearances to various followers;

3. forgiveness extended to these followers who had deserted Jesus and fled;
4. commissioning to go tell the good news of the resurrection and carry on the mission of Jesus.

In addition, we can underline these aspects of the resurrection accounts:

1. Mary Magdalene was there at the tomb in all four Gospels, the one constant figure.
2. Jesus' resurrection body was not a resuscitated corpse, nor was it a ghost. Then and now, it is something else, transcending space and time, recognizable and unrecognizable.
3. The resurrection appearances did not command automatic belief; there was doubt and faith, joy and disbelief.
4. Something happened to Jesus, not just to the disciples. Resurrection appearances were more than a subjective, hallucinatory experience or grief reaction in the disciples' inner world. Jesus was raised by God from the dead.
5. Some of the appearances seem uniquely tailored for different disciples: Mary Magdalene, Peter, Thomas, Paul.
6. The resurrection appearance to Paul, which happened about eighteen months after these first appearances, was different. Christ appeared from heaven, in the heavens, not on earth. It was a vision with both visionary and auditory dimensions. It is closer to the kinds of experiences people will have with the more-than-historical Jesus throughout the centuries.

The resurrection of Jesus is neither provable nor disprovable by modern scientific or historical methods. It lies in the realm of spiritual encounter. Now, as then, it invites faith; it does not coerce faith. It was an event within history that had a historical impact on the disciples so great that Christianity is unimaginable without it.

To those who received and believed the resurrection encounters, Jesus promised two things: (1) the power of God's Spirit to help his followers on their mission in Jesus' name, and (2) to be with them always.

Here is the Christian experience: Christ is present to believers through the Spirit of God. Encounters with the Risen Christ have happened in worship, around the Communion table in the Eucharist, in acts of love and service, and in relationship with the "least of these" in whom Jesus waits for us. They have happened to believers and unbelievers outside church as well as inside church.

The arc of the Jesus Story—of the historical Jesus and the more-than-historical Jesus—includes his conception and birth, his life and ministry, the cross and, yes, the resurrection. The words of the poet Gerard Manley Hopkins speak the longing and hope of his followers:

> *Let him easter in us, be a dayspring to the dimness of us, be a*
> *crimson-cresseted east,*
> *More brightening [us] . . . as his reign rolls.*[4]

NOTES

1. Modern historians require "objective" corroboration from those outside the circle of believers. They also maintain a suspicion, if not dismissal, of "supernatural" happenings.

2. Mark's longer ending, not in the earliest manuscripts, contains an allusion to this story (Mark 16:12-13).

3. Denise Levertov, "St. Thomas Didymus," in Denise Levertov, *Selected Poems* (New York: New Directions, 2002), 170.

4. Gerard Manley Hopkins, "The Wreck of the Deutschland," in Gerard Manley Hopkins, *Poems and Prose* (New York: Penguin Books, 1963), 24.

PART V

CONCLUSIONS

25

WHO IS JESUS CHRIST FOR US TODAY?

What shall I say as we conclude this phase of our search for the historical and more-than-historical Jesus? The search will go on and on. It will never in this life be completed. Dietrich Bonhoeffer once said that the most crucial question about Jesus is "Who is Jesus Christ for us today?" *Who* is the question of personal response. The ball is in our court.

Who was Jesus for Israel? Who is he for us? Who is he for the world? According to a 2011 study of more than two hundred countries, there are an estimated 2.18 billion Christians in the world, representing nearly a third of the 2010 global population of 6.9 billion.[1] Jesus is of staggering significance to the world.

There have been three scholarly quests for the historical Jesus. The first quest bridged the late nineteenth and early twentieth centuries. The second quest was in the 1950s and 1960s. The third quest began in the 1980s and continues to this day. In between have been periods where scholars believed there was little scientific historical knowledge of Jesus to be found. During these times, scholars such as Rudolph Bultmann emphasized the existential encounter with Christ, both then and now.

My exploration has identified what we can reasonably know about the figure Jesus of Nazareth. He has not only inspired the 2.18 billion Christians today, but also he has inspired many who do not call themselves Christian. Gandhi is but one significant example.

Who *is* Jesus Christ for us today? Poet Anne Sexton wished to know that "the Christ who walked for me / walked on true ground."[2] It is also important to know that the Christ who walked on true ground walked for us.

GOD WITH US, FOR US, AHEAD OF US

Author and pastor Rob Bell says that there are three qualities about God that are crucial for our spiritual lives: God is *with* us; God is *for* us; and God is *ahead of* us. That is, God is pulling us forward toward deeper, truer relationship with God and toward a better, more just, and healing world.[3]

During his ministry on earth, Jesus embodied these three qualities of God and revealed them to us in and through his life. He was God-with-us, God-for-us, and God-ahead-of-us.

There is a foundational syntax used by the church throughout the world and throughout the centuries. The Nicene Creed expressed it this way: Jesus died for us and our salvation. What can such words mean for us today? God is with us, for us, and ahead of us. Let's explore.

GOD WITH US

Jesus came to reveal that God is Immanuel, God *with* us, in all life's circumstances, good and ill, beautiful and terrible. He taught us to trust in God's goodness and in what theologian Oscar Cullmann called the "faithfulness at the heart of all things."[4] Recall Jesus' invitation to "consider the lilies" (Luke 12:27). With God we experience the wonder and beauty of life.

In Christ we also experience that God is with us in the worst of circumstances. Peter Kreeft, a professor of philosophy, writes:

He came. He entered space and time and suffering. He came, like a lover. . . . He sits beside us in the lowest places of our lives, like water. Are we broken? He is broken with us. Are we rejected? . . . He was "despised and rejected of men." . . . Do we weep? . . . He was "a man of sorrows and acquainted with grief." . . . Does he descend into all our hells? Yes. In the unforgettable line of Corrie ten Boom from the depths of a Nazi death camp, "No matter how deep our darkness, he is deeper still."[5]

GOD FOR US

Jesus taught and embodied God *for* us. This "for" language is part of the deep syntax of Christian faith. Jesus died for us and our salvation.

This language need not be tied to a theology of blood atonement, where God required the death of his Son, Jesus, in order for us to be forgiven and saved. Indeed, for many today, we must separate such "for-ness" from such theology. And yet, the for-ness of God in Jesus is a sublime truth not to be discarded.

First of all, we begin by saying that Jesus *lived* for us and our salvation. His preaching and embodiment of the kingdom of God were for our healing and wholeness and for the healing and wholeness of the world. Such is the core meaning of the word *salvation*.

Second, we may say that his life was *given*, every moment of it, including most powerfully his death. His death was a life *given*, not *taken*, nor *required*. His life was a life poured out for us from its beginning to its end. Jesus said, "For the Son of Man also came not to be served but to serve, and to give his life as a ransom for many" (Mark 10:45). "Ransom" was a word that meant "liberation": "release to captives . . . liberty to the oppressed" (Luke 4:18) was his aim.

His life *given* has been an inspiration and a template for the lives of those who have followed him. Bill Wilson, cofounder of Alcoholics Anonymous, arrived at an essential truth in his own battle with alcoholism: the only way to stay sober was to be about the daily work of helping other alcoholics. Martin Luther King Jr.'s life was a life *given* for the cause of justice and reconciliation. Dorothy Day's and Mother Teresa's lives were lives *given* for the poor in New York City and Calcutta. Father Damien was a priest who went to minister in a leper colony on the island of Molokai and contracted leprosy himself. His was a life *given* for the lepers in the Spirit of Christ.

Christians throughout two millennia have been captivated by the self-giving love of Christ and have sought to pass that love. The church, when it has truly been the church, has been what author and theologian Barbara Brown Taylor has called a "poured-out church."

One of the most dramatic examples of a life *given* was the life of Christian de Chergé, a Trappist monk serving the Muslim people of Algeria.[6] (His story was portrayed in the 2010 film *Of Gods and Men*.)

On May 26, 1996, Christian's mother opened a sealed letter containing the last words of her son, who had just been beheaded by a militant Muslim group, Groupe Islamique Armé (GIA). The GIA had taken control of much of the country and demanded that all foreigners leave. Christian de Chergé, the prior of the Trappist monastery in the region, who had spent virtually his whole life among the people of Algeria, refused to leave.

He had grown up from boyhood there, the son of a French military man stationed in Algeria. He grew to love the Algerian people and have deep respect for their Muslim faith. He would observe the reverence of their worship and lives. His mother told him that he must always respect them because they worshiped the same God. De Chergé called his mother his "very first church."

But there was another transformative moment in his life. It happened in 1959 while de Chergé was serving in the military in Algeria. He developed a close friendship with a local village policeman named Mohamed. One evening, as they were walking along, Christian was accosted by a violent group. Mohamed intervened and rescued his friend, and the next day Mohamed was assassinated. Christian had seen "the soul of Islam" in his friend and recognized its kinship with the soul of Christianity. Mohamed had the spirit of Christian's own Jesus, who said, "No one has greater love than this, to lay down one's life for one's friends" (John 15:13, NRSV). So later, when the GIA demanded that de Chergé leave the Muslim people he loved, he refused.

When his mother opened the letter, she read these words:

> If it should happen one day—it could be today—that I have become a victim of the terrorism which now seems ready to engulf all the foreigners living in Algeria, I would like my community, my church, my family to remember that my life was GIVEN [note his capital letters] to God and to this country.

The last portion of the letter was written to his prospective murderer looming on the horizon:

> And also to you, the friend of the final moment, who would not be aware of what you were doing. Yes, I also say this THANK YOU and A DIEU to you in whom I see the face of God.
>
> And we may find each other, happy thieves in Paradise, if it pleases God, the Father of us both. Amen. In sha 'Allah.

Merci, thank you, he wrote, and *adieu*, a good-bye blessing, "to God," lifting him into the merciful hands of God. Then *amen*, so let it be, and finally the Muslim phrase used daily, *In sha 'Allah*, God willing.

We can see how Christ's life and death were imprinted on Christian's own life and death, his life as Christ's own life *GIVEN* for us.

GOD AHEAD OF US

Third, Jesus reveals that God is God *ahead of* us. The "theology of hope" popularized in the 1970s pictured God not so much above us coming down to us as ahead of us, coming to us from the future.

When the angel in Mark's Gospel commissioned the women to go tell the glad news of Easter, he said, "Go, tell his disciples and Peter that he is going before you to Galilee; there you will see him" (Mark 16:7).

As God is ahead of us, drawing us into the life of God today and toward God's dream for the world, Jesus is also going ahead of us, inviting us to follow, enter the kingdom of God, and discover what God is doing in our time.

Again, Albert Schweitzer's words, the final paragraph of his *The Quest of the Historical Jesus*, lead us on:

> He comes to us as One unknown. . . . He speaks to us the same word: "Follow thou me!" and sets us to the tasks which he has to fulfill for our time. He commands. And to those who obey Him . . . He will reveal Himself. . . . And, as an ineffable mystery, they shall learn in their own experience Who He is.[7]

CONCLUSION

In the brilliant and startling light of the resurrection, a shift occurred. The message *of* Jesus (i.e., his sayings and teachings) shifted to the message *about* Jesus, primarily about his birth, death, and resurrection.

The Apostles' Creed jumps from "born of the Virgin Mary" to "suffered under Pontius Pilate." What about his life, ministry, and message? The quest for the historical Jesus, along with close attention to the Gospels, help to fill in the gap. In the best theology about Christ there is a deep correlation between the message *of* Jesus and the message *about* Jesus. The message of the historical Jesus is captured in the words "The kingdom of God is *entos* you," within you, among you, in your midst. The message about Jesus—and here I speak of the more-than-historical Jesus—is *Jesus* is *entos* you, within you, among you, in your midst. As we combine the search for the historical Jesus and more-than-historical Jesus, we will learn more clearly who Jesus Christ is for us today.

There are few hymns written about the historical Jesus, his life and message. More hymns are penned about Christ's theological significance or are written *to* Christ. I took this as a challenge and wrote the following hymn about the historical Jesus a few years ago while hiking in the mountains of North Carolina and later that year on Iona's sacred soil. As I wrote, I hummed the tune *Lauda anima*.

> *Praise the one who came among us,*
> *God's own child from Galilee.*
> *Home he was in field and temple,*
> *Romping in his Abba's glee.*
> *Alleluia, alleluia, Praise the boy from Galilee.*
>
> *Praise the Son at his baptism,*
> *God's true servant he would be.*
> *He would work his Abba's pleasure:*
> *Healing, justice, liberty.*
> *Alleluia, alleluia, Washed, anointed, Spirit-freed.*
>
> *When he preached his hometown sermon,*
> *Some rose up to kill him then.*
> *He announced the kingdom's nearness*
> *Come alike to foe and friend.*
> *Alleluia, alleluia, Praise the prophets who offend.*
>
> *Jesus ate with cast-out sinners,*
> *He made holy unclean things,*
> *Teaching grace that springs to meet us,*

Bringing healing in its wings.
Alleluia, alleluia, Love makes whole all broken things.

"Sell your wealth; away now give it
To the poor, then follow me.
Bless them who have harmed and hurt you.
Do all this, and you'll be free."
Alleluia, alleluia, Hear the Freeing One's decrees.

Christ turned over greed's full tables
Set up in the house of God.
"This, God's house, is for all people,"
House of prayer and praise to all.
Alleluia, alleluia, Open now God's gates to all.

Jesus strode to Calv'ry's mountain,
Poured his life out for us all.
Then God raised him Easter's morning,
Love defeating death's dark thrall.
Alleluia, alleluia, Christ is risen for us all.

NOTES

1. Pew Research Center, "Global Christianity—A Report on the Size and Distribution of the World's Christian Population," December 19, 2011, Pewforum.org/2011/12/19/global-christianity-exec/.

2. Anne Sexton, "Frenzy," in Anne Sexton, *The Complete Poems* (Boston: Houghton Mifflin, 1981), 466.

3. See Rob Bell, *What We Talk About When We Talk About God* (New York: HarperOne, 2013), 97–174.

4. Quoted by David Steindl-Rast, *Gratefulness, the Heart Prayer: An Approach to Life in Fullness* (New York: Paulist Press, 1984), 102.

5. Peter Kreeft, *Making Sense Out of Suffering* (Ann Arbor, MI: Servant Books, 1986), 133–34.

6. I am indebted to Karl Plank for this story. See Karl Plank, "When an A-Dieu Takes on a Face: The Last Testament of Christian de Chergé, O.C.S.O," *Spiritual Life* 53, no. 3 (2007): 136–47.

7. Albert Schweitzer, *The Quest of the Historical Jesus: A Critical Study of Its Progress from Reimarus to Wrede* (Baltimore: Johns Hopkins University Press, with the Albert Schweitzer Institute, 1998), 403.

EPILOGUE

The Ninety-Nine Names
of Jesus

Early in John's Gospel, Jesus is being named, and he is naming others (John 1:29-51). Naming or being named is a sacred act. In ancient cultures and in the Bible, the naming of a child is of great importance, often marked by ritual. Renaming is important too—for example, Jacob, renamed Israel; Sarai, renamed Sarah; Simon, renamed Peter. Sometimes a new name is given when one converts to a new faith or enters a monastery.

NAMING IN JOHN'S GOSPEL

John the Baptist saw Jesus coming toward him and said, "Behold, the Lamb of God, who takes away the sin of the world" (John 1:29).

The next day John, flanked by two disciples, saw Jesus passing by and said again, "Behold, the Lamb of God." John's disciples followed after Jesus to see what he was about.

When Jesus saw them, he turned and asked, "What do you seek? What are you looking for?" They named Jesus "Rabbi, Teacher" and asked, "Where are you staying?"

In John's Gospel, dialogue is almost always double layered. The question is more than "Where are you spending the night?" The Jerusalem Hilton? Mary's house? It means

"Where do you come from?" John had already provided the answer earlier: Jesus came from the heart of God, from the bosom of the Father (John 1:18).

Jesus did not reply directly to their question but said enticingly, "Come and see." One of the two disciples happened to be Andrew, brother of Simon, who rushed to his brother and said, "We have found the Christ," or "Messiah," which in the Hebrew means "Anointed One." Andrew then hauled his brother to meet Jesus, and Jesus said to him, "So, you are Simon, son of John. You shall be called Cephas, or Peter, which means 'Rock.'"

There is double naming going on—in this text and in our lives. We name Jesus, and Jesus names us. We are discerning who he is, and he is revealing who we are.

The next day, Jesus went to Galilee, found a man named Philip, and said to him, "Follow me." Philip went to his friend Nathanael and said, "We have found the one about whom Moses and the prophets wrote: Jesus of Nazareth."

Nathanael scoffed, "Can anything good come out of Nazareth?" (Supply the name of your city of choice.) Now, it was Philip who invited, "Come and see." Jesus saw Nathanael coming and said, "Behold, an Israelite in whom there is no guile," which essentially meant, in this guy, what you see is what you get.

Nathanael asked, "How do you know me?" Jesus answered, "Before Philip called you, when you were under the fig tree, I saw you." In effect, I know you better than you know yourself.

Nathanael responded, "Rabbi, you are the son of God, the king of Israel." Jesus then said, "You will see angels ascending and descending upon the Son of Man." In other words, Jesus is Jacob's ladder, heaven's gate.

There is a multiplicity of names for Jesus in this one passage, a multiplicity that reveals who Jesus is, but by its multiplicity preserves the mystery of who he is.

Lamb of God
Rabbi, Teacher
Messiah, or Christ
One about Whom Moses and the Prophets Wrote
Jesus of Nazareth
Son of God
King of Israel
Jacob's Ladder, Heaven's Gate
Son of Man

Nine names.

Muslim and Sufi spirituality have ninety-nine names for God. The ninety-nine names describe who God is, and the number ninety-nine signifies that an infinite number of names for the infinite God.

THE NINETY-NINE NAMES OF JESUS

Here are some names for Jesus, ninety-nine names or clusters of names, in roughly alphabetical order. They come from the Bible, from sacred poetry, hymns, liturgy, and mystical experiences of Jesus through the centuries. As Charles Wesley wrote, "O for a thousand tongues to sing my great Redeemer's praise."

NINETY-NINE NAMES OF JESUS

Abba's Child
Alpha and Omega
Anointed One
Balm of Gilead
Beautiful Savior
Beloved
Blossom, Dawn, Dew on the Grass
Bread of Life
Bridegroom
Brother
Center
Christ
Cup of Forgiveness
Darling Jesus
Deliverer
Door
Dreamer

Emmanuel, Immanuel,
    God-with-us
Exiled King
Fairest of Ten Thousand
Fisherman
Forgotten Revelation
Friend
Friend of Outcasts and
    Sinners
Friend of the Poor
Fully Human One
Gardener
Gate of Heaven
God's Favorite Story
Good Shepherd
Great Physician
Heaven's Harmonies, God's
    Song
Hope of the Hopeless
Humanity of God
Icon, or Image of God
Ihidaya, Single One, Unified
    One, Integrated One
Inner Light
Jesus, *Yeshua* (which means
    "Yahweh saves")
Jesus of Nazareth
Joy of Our Desiring
King of Kings
King of My Heart
Lamb of God
Last of the Great Detectives
Liberator
Light of the World
Lily of the Valley
Living Water

Lord
Lord of the Dance
Love Itself
Lover of My Soul
Love's Bitten Tongue,
    Heaven's Wound
Man of Sorrows
Mediator
Misfit
Model
Mother
My Great Dignity
My Sweet Lord
Mystery Made Flesh
Mystic River
One about Whom Moses
    and the Prophets Wrote
One Who Is Coming into the
    World
Parable of God
Peace, Peace of God, Prince
    of Peace
Pearl of Great Price
Pioneer, Trail-Blazer,
    Path-Finder
Ploughman Who Becomes
    the Wheat, Winepress
    That Becomes the Wine
Poem of God
Presence of the Kingdom
Priest
Prophet
Rabbi
Radiance, Incendiary
Redeemer
Resurrection and the Life

Revealer, Revelator
Risen One, Living One
Sacrament of God
Savior
Second Adam
Servant
Servant of God
Servant of the Poor
Son of God
Son of Man
Son of Mary, Joseph's Boy
Suffering Servant
Surprise of Mercy, Outgo-
    ing Gladness, Rescue,
    Healing and Life
Symbol of God
Teacher
Treasure
Tree of Life
Vine
Volunteer
The Way, the Truth, the Life
Wisdom of God
Word of God

May the names and the naming never end.

INDEX